ATHENS BURNING

WITNESS TO ANCIENT HISTORY

GREGORY S. ALDRETE, *Series Editor*

ALSO IN THE SERIES

Jerry Toner, *The Day Commodus Killed a Rhino:
Understanding the Roman Games*

Debra Hamel, *The Battle of Arginusae: Victory at Sea
and Its Tragic Aftermath in the Final Years
of the Peloponnesian War*

ATHENS BURNING

The Persian Invasion of Greece
and the Evacuation of Attica

Robert Garland
COLGATE UNIVERSITY

Johns Hopkins University Press
Baltimore

© 2017 Johns Hopkins University Press
All rights reserved. Published 2017
Printed in the United States of America on acid-free paper
2   4   6   8   9   7   5   3   1

Johns Hopkins University Press
2715 North Charles Street
Baltimore, Maryland 21218-4363
www.press.jhu.edu

Library of Congress Cataloging-in-Publication Data

Names: Garland, Robert, 1947–, author.
Title: Athens Burning : the Persian invasion of Greece and the evacuation
of Attica / Robert Garland.
Description: Baltimore : Johns Hopkins University Press, 2017. |
Series: Witness to ancient history | Includes bibliographical references
and index.
Identifiers: LCCN 2016022026| ISBN 9781421421957 (hardcover :
alk. paper) | ISBN 142142195X (hardcover : alk. paper) | ISBN
9781421421964 (pbk. : alk. paper) | ISBN 1421421968 (pbk. : alk. paper) |
ISBN 9781421421971 (electronic) | ISBN 1421421976 (electronic)
Subjects: LCSH: Athens (Greece)—History—Siege, 480 B.C. | Greece—
History—Persian Wars, 500-449 B.C.—Social aspects. | Civilians
in war—Greece—Athens—History—To 1500. | Greece—History—
Persian Wars, 500-449 B.C.—Campaigns.
Classification: LCC DF225.55 .G37 2017 | DDC 938/.03—dc23
LC record available at https://lccn.loc.gov/2016022026

A catalog record for this book is available from the British Library.

Special discounts are available for bulk purchases of this book.
For more information, please contact Special Sales at 410-516-6936
or specialsales@press.jhu.edu.

Johns Hopkins University Press uses environmentally friendly book
materials, including recycled text paper that is composed of at least
30 percent post-consumer waste, whenever possible.

For Richard and Danielle with love

*Une même vague par le monde, une même vague depuis Troie roule
sa hanche jusqu'à nous.*

Saint-John Perse

•

I hope they will not forget the poor devils that died here.

Sapper Harry Billinge on the seventy-year commemoration of D-Day
(June 6, 2014)

CONTENTS

ILLUSTRATIONS

TIMELINE

490
Winter

Following the Persian defeat at Marathon, Darius I gives orders to make preparations for another expedition.

486
September/October

The accession of Xerxes I follows the death of Darius I.

484
By the end of the year

Xerxes crushes revolts in Egypt and Babylon.

483
Summer

On Themistocles' recommendation, the Athenians devote the silver accruing from their silver mines at Laurium to building a fleet of two hundred triremes. Xerxes begins preparations for an invasion of Greece; his engineers start digging a canal though the neck of the peninsula at Mount Athos.

481
April/May

Xerxes sets out from Susa.

September/October

Xerxes arrives in Sardis. He sends envoys to Greece demanding submission. At least thirty-one Greek states meet at Sparta and form an alliance to resist the Persians. The Athenians consult the Delphic Oracle. They vote to abandon Attica and resist the Persians at sea.

| October/November or later | The Athenians pass the Decree of Themistocles and begin an orderly evacuation. |

480

April	Xerxes marches from Sardis with his army.
May	Xerxes crosses the Hellespont. The Greeks march north to the Vale of Tempe but withdraw to the Isthmus of Corinth soon afterward.
Early summer	The Athenian fleet of two hundred triremes is ready.
End of August	The battles of Thermopylae and Artemisium are fought.
End of August/ early September	The Athenians conduct an emergency evacuation from Attica.
Early September	The Persian advance guard enters Attica.
Mid- to late September	The Persian army enters Athens. The Persian fleet moors at Phaleron. Shortly afterward the Acropolis falls. Xerxes sets fire to Athens. The Peloponnesian army marches to the Isthmus of Corinth. Work begins on building a wall across the isthmus.
	The Battle of Salamis is fought.
Early October	The Persian navy sets sail from Phaleron and begins its voyage back to the Hellespont. The Athenian navy sets off in pursuit. A day or two later Xerxes begins his march back to Persia. Soon afterward the Athenian evacuees begin returning from Salamis.

479

| February | Themistocles fails to be elected to the board of generals for the year July 479–June 478. |
| March/April | Mardonius sends Alexander of Macedon to Salamis to propose peace terms with the Athenians. |

May	The Athenians undertake a second evacuation from Attica.
Late June	Mardonius invades Attica. He sends a Greek, Mourychides, across to Salamis with an offer of peace terms. After the Athenians reject the offer, Mardonius sets fire to the city.
July	Mardonius departs from Attica.
August	The Battle of Plataea is fought.

Prologue

IF YOU WALK from Syntagma Square, where the Greek parliament building stands, down modern Odhos Hermou as the road passes through the industrial district on the west side of Athens, you will eventually come to the chief burial ground of the ancient city. The Ceramicus, or Potters' District, as it is called, lies just outside the circuit wall, which is pierced at this point by two major gates. Modern historians refer to it as the Themistoclean Wall, in deference to the politician and general Themistocles, who urged the Athenians to construct it hastily after the defeat of the Persians at the Battle of Plataea in August 479. They did so following the return of the civilian population, which had evacuated in advance of the Persian army led by King Xerxes.[1]

The wall was built largely out of debris resulting from the double burning of Athens in 480 and 479. From the exposed section of the wall beside the two city gates, you can still today identify many fragments of funerary monuments that the Athenians utilized in its construction. This recycling of high-quality sculpture is indicative of the unsentimental, no-nonsense policy that the Athenians adopted at the end of a war that had seen their city burned not once but twice within a single year. The determination to preserve their freedom at all costs outweighed any other consideration, and for this reason everyone shared in the labor—men, women, and children alike. In my view, it is one of the greatest

The Themistoclean Wall

community building projects ever undertaken and, once completed, it set Athens firmly on the path to full democracy.

This book takes its inspiration from the sufferings of those tens of thousands of Athenian refugees who chose to abandon their homes, their ancestral tombs, and their shrines, without any certainty they would ever return. It was a fate that millions have repeated throughout history. Women and children were sent to one safe haven, the elderly to another, while the men of military age were conscripted into the fleet.

There are many books on the Persian wars, but battles are not my chief focus. Rather, what interests me is the fate of the civilians during the three or four months that preceded the arrival of the Persians and the ten months that followed before their departure—the period from June 480 to August 479, to be precise—when the population took first to the road and then to the sea, seeking refuge abroad.

The decision on the part of the Athenians to become refugees rather than defend their city raises many questions of a logistical nature. How was the evacuation organized? What facilities were provided at staging posts along the way?

How were the evacuees transported out of Attica? What happened to the slaves? Emotions, mainly off limits for ancient historians, are a constant undercurrent—the fearful anticipation before the invasion of Xerxes, the anxiety close to panic in advance of his arrival, the tense expectancy on the eve of the Battle of Salamis, the relief at the outcome of the battle tempered by the trauma upon returning to discover tombs, temples, and homes reduced to rubble, the impotent fury at having to undertake a second evacuation less than a year after the first, and the misery on returning to discover that whatever they had been able to repair was again broken and burned.

The perspective of Xerxes' army is also important, even though there isn't any reference to the invasion in any extant Persian text. After all, every war is an argument, so to speak, between two or more cultures. And it is always vital to ask pertinent—and impertinent—questions, even if hard data are lacking. What was Xerxes' intention when he took the decision to invade Greece? What knowledge did he have of Athens or its people? What did his soldiers and sailors know of the country they were invading? And when Xerxes withdrew from Greece with the larger part of his army after suffering a catastrophic defeat at Salamis, how demoralized did his army feel? I end with a chapter devoted to the aftermath of the invasion, when the Athenians dug themselves out of the rubble and sought to construct an interpretation of the reasons for their survival.

Many ancient historians see the Greco-Persian Wars as a "clash of civilizations" with the right side, that is, "us," winning, and Western civilization surviving and flourishing as a result. It can hardly be denied that Western civilization in general and Greek civilization in particular benefited greatly from the Persian defeat. Even so, it's important not to be too dewy-eyed. The Greeks were fighting for their survival, not for any ideal. Most of their decisions were governed by narrow self-interest. Both they and the Persians committed acts of despicable barbarity. And finally, many Greek communities did not fight against the Persians, while many others were compelled to fight on the Persian side. It's also vital not to fall victim to the stereotypical image of the Persian king as a brutal and bloodthirsty tyrant—an image that derives as much from modern interpretations as it does from the historical Greek tradition.

-I-

The Origins

The Athenians and the Others

At the time of King Xerxes' invasion of Greece in 480 BCE, the Persian Empire—also known as the Achaemenid Empire after Achaemenes, the legendary founder of the imperial dynasty—extended over the entire Near East, from Pakistan in the east, to Egypt in the south, from Macedonia in the west, to the Black Sea and Caucasus Mountains in the north. Or, to put it rather differently, it included all of modern-day Iran, Iraq, Kuwait, Turkey, Afghanistan, Israel, Palestine, Jordan, Armenia, Azerbaijan, and Georgia, as well as parts of Egypt, Libya, Bulgaria, Romania, Russia, Ukraine, and Greece.

What makes this all the more remarkable is that the phenomenal rise of Persia occurred in the space of barely half a century, mainly under Cyrus II, who is otherwise known as Cyrus the Great (r. 559–530). Cyrus, king of Anshan, a region in southwestern Iran that includes modern-day Shiraz, first conquered the Medes, then the Lydians and Asiatic Greeks, and next the Neo-Babylonians. Originally cattle herders, the Persians are thought to have migrated from central Asia into the modern-day Iranian province of Fars (known in Old Persian as Parsa, hence our word "Persia"), where they acculturated with a local people known as the Elamites. They had for centuries been overshadowed, first by the

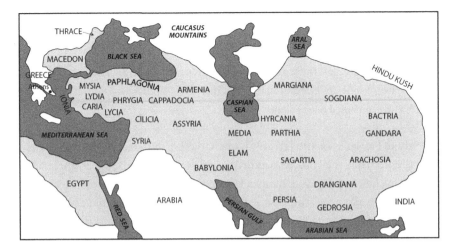

The Persian Empire

Neo-Assyrians and then by the Neo-Babylonians. By the time of the Greco-Persian Wars they were "highly advanced, heirs to and innovators in civilizations that predated the Greeks by centuries."[1]

Their empire was first divided into twenty provinces known as satrapies, later raised to twenty-three by King Darius I (r. 522–486). Each province was ruled by a satrap (literally "protector of the kingdom") or viceroy, who collected taxes and acted as the ultimate arbiter of the judicial system. It incorporated a multitude of different peoples, which made it the world's first truly multiethnic, polyglot empire. It covered about a million square miles, though some scholars estimate that it was considerably larger. The size of its population is impossible to gauge. The low estimate is 17 million, the high between 30 and 35 million.[2] It became the largest empire the world had yet seen, and it would remain the largest until 330 BCE, when it was conquered by Alexander the Great. The claim put forward by the chorus in Aeschylus's *Persians* that Persia's dominance in Asia was "destroyed" as a result of Xerxes' defeat is entirely without foundation. The Greco-Persian Wars in no way diminished Persia's influence worldwide—an essential fact to bear in mind in any assessment of the significance of Greece's victory.[3] Robert Graves got it right in his poem "The Persian Version"—the Persian version, that is, of the battles of Marathon and Salamis:

> Truth-loving Persians do not dwell upon
> The trivial skirmish fought near Marathon.
> As for the Greek theatrical tradition

Which represents that summer's expedition
Not as a mere reconnaissance in force . . .
But as a grandiose, ill-starred attempt
To conquer Greece—they treat it with contempt . . .
Despite a strong defence and adverse weather
All arms combined magnificently together.

Ethnic Persians constituted only a small fraction of the total population. Unlike the Romans, they made no effort to impose their way of life on their subjects. On the contrary, as Johannes Haubold has aptly commented, "Much of the time, the aim was rather to create a hybrid discourse that could accommodate both imperial and local concerns."[4] So far as we can tell, their rule was relatively benign. Babylonians, Greeks, Egyptians, and others managed their local affairs, were permitted to worship their own gods, followed their own customs, and spoke their own languages. The king issued pronouncements in Aramaic, which was the official language of Persian diplomacy, as well as in local languages. Thus, the author (or authors) of the book of Esther in the Hebrew Bible tells us that the King Ahasuerus (a name identified with Xerxes, quite possibly the same Xerxes who led the expedition against Greece) sent word "to every province in its own script and to every people in their own language." So if you'd been an Edomite or a Lycian or a Carian, it's a fair bet that you wouldn't have found Persian overlordship particularly irksome, so long as you didn't do anything reckless, such as trying to revolt, in which case the Persian response would be ruthless. It would include being subjected to exacting penalties, such as impalement. Even so, it may well be, as John Boardman observes, that the Persians "exhibited perhaps a little less of the sheer cruelty displayed by many ancient peoples, including the Greeks."[5]

The obligations to which subjects were bound included service in the army. In addition, each satrapy had to pay taxes according to its kind. The Bactrians contributed gold and camels, the Saka clothes and horses, the Sogdians lapis lazuli and carnelian, and so on. Much of the empire was urbanized, and Babylon was probably the largest city in the world at the time of Xerxes' invasion—larger than any other city in Mesopotamia and larger than all the Greek cities in western Anatolia. Many of the nobility, however, lived on large estates that were provided with ornamental gardens and parklands. Our word "paradise" derives from the Old Persian word *paridaida*, meaning "enclosure, park." The nobility benefited greatly from the riches that accrued to them as a result of taxation.

At the head of the empire was the king, with the power of life and death over his subjects. If we are to believe Herodotus, the king chiefly exercised his power over his immediate entourage, including his generals. We rarely hear of him executing commoners. Though he was assisted in his deliberations by advisers, many of whom were relatives, he was answerable to no one. The Persian army, like the empire, functioned as an autocracy. This means that his advisers did little more than form "an echo-chamber for the king's policies."[6] An interesting example is when Artemisia, queen of Halicarnassus, urges Xerxes to avoid the naval battle at Salamis. Her fellow generals expect her to be severely punished for speaking out of line. Paradoxically, Xerxes was allegedly delighted with her reply, though in the end he chose to ignore it.

Though the king's word was law, Herodotus would have us believe that there were some highly placed Persians who disapproved of Xerxes' decision to invade Greece and who "rejoiced and prostrated themselves" when he announced that he had abandoned his plan.[7] On the eve of the Battle of Plataea, an unnamed Persian spoke bitterly of the fact that, though defeat was staring them in the face, he and his compatriots were "constrained by necessity to follow orders." He added: "No pain is more hateful than to have profound understanding and be incapable of acting upon it."[8] It is a sentiment that to a Greek strongly smacks of what is sometimes called oriental despotism.

The king was attended by a small group of religious officials known as *magoi* (our word "magician"). Herodotus suggests that the *magoi* played a decisive role in persuading Xerxes to undertake the invasion of Greece by informing him that a dream that he reported to them indicated that "all those on earth would become his slaves."[9] This is not much more credible than his claim that Atossa sought to incite her husband Darius I to invade Greece because she wanted to acquire Spartan women as slaves.[10] How frequently Xerxes took the advice of the *magoi* on campaign is debatable.

The most prominent deity in the pantheon was Ahura-Mazda, the upholder of justice and truth, who was in a perpetual battle with the spirits of darkness, one of the chief of whom was Ahriman. Ahura-Mazda is said to have been elevated to the rank of principal deity by a Persian sage called Zarathustra, also known as Zoroaster. Zoroaster's dates are uncertain, but he may have lived as early as 1000 BCE. The king was Ahura-Mazda's regent or representative on earth. Though not a god himself, he required all his subjects and all foreigners to kneel before him. Because the Greeks viewed kneeling as an act of worship, they thought that the Persians actually worshiped their king as a god. This misunderstanding would be a source of conflict and confusion between the two peoples that would last for hundreds of years.

Whether Ahura-Mazda served all the people living within the empire is unclear.[11] As in the Greek world, there were many hundreds, if not thousands, of local deities, specific to individual peoples and particular regions. The Persians permitted the worship of these local deities to continue and, in some cases, even began worshiping them themselves. The most striking example of Persian acceptance of foreign religion has to do with the Jews. When Cyrus the Great conquered Babylon in 539, he acceded to a petition from a group of Jewish exiles who wished to return to their homeland to worship their one god, Yahweh. Had he not done so, Judaism, as we know it today, might have remained an insignificant "cult," and Christianity might never have grown out of it, or Islam out of both.[12]

Despite similarities, the contrasts between the Persians and the Greeks were numerous. The Greeks were divided into independent *poleis*, or city-states, of various sizes, of which Athens was the largest in terms of population. It is conceivable that there were as many as 1,035 *poleis* in existence when the Greek world was at its demographic height, but "lack of sources makes it impossible to draw a picture of the *polis* world in the year of Xerxes' invasion of Greece," as Mogens Hansen and Thomas Nielsen judiciously note in their definitive study of the *polis*.[13]

Plato memorably likens the Greeks to "frogs around a pond," the pond in question being the Mediterranean and Black Sea, around whose coastline they established hundreds of settlements. There were city-states in what today are Albania, Bulgaria, Egypt, France, Georgia, Italy, Sicily, Spain, Turkey, and Ukraine. Each had its own law code, its own political system, its own socioeconomic structure, and its own religious observances. Each fiercely guarded its independence. Most were ruled by aristocracies or oligarchies. In 480 Athens was unusual but not unique in already being a fledgling democracy.

Though the Greeks acknowledged a common ancestry (albeit from four separate branches known as Ionian, Dorian, Aeolian, and Achaean), spoke a common language (albeit with dialectal variants), worshiped common gods (albeit with local variants), and maintained a common culture (albeit in highly distinctive ways), they were incessantly at war with one another. As Simon Hornblower has observed, the onomatopoeic word *phthonos*, meaning "jealousy, malice, rivalry, envy, grudge," accurately epitomizes the type of relationship that often existed between one *polis* and another.[14] The kind of hostility to which this gave rise had no clear or certain origin and no real hope of ultimate resolution.

It festered and it rankled. As a result of their cherished differences, the Greeks saw themselves primarily as Athenians or Spartans or Corinthians or Thebans, and as Greeks or Hellēnes, as they called themselves, only a distant second. At the time of Xerxes' invasion of Greece, Athens had been at war with Aegina for more than twenty years. It was an interminable and pointless conflict and, like so many others, had its roots in *phthonos.*

It took an outside threat, like that presented by the Persians, to bring the Greeks into dialogue with one another. However, even under conditions of extreme duress, when survival depended on unified action, each *polis* made decisions based primarily on its own self-interest rather than on the common good. Whenever the Greeks sought to engage in collective action, sharp divisions threatened to shatter their unity. In fact, freedom—their essential watchword and one they proudly touted—meant freedom not to have to act in the common good as much as it meant freedom from foreign oppression. As Herodotus points out, the only reason why the Phocians, a people who lived in central Greece, remained loyal to the Greek cause during the Greco-Persian Wars was because they hated their neighbors, the Thessalians, who had sided with the Persians. Had the Thessalians supported the Greeks, the Phocians would have joined the Persians.[15] Rancor doesn't run much deeper than that.

A *polis* consisted of an urban center surrounded by countryside. The extent of territory owned by each was delimited by mountains, sea, or proximity to another city-state. Attica, the countryside surrounding Athens, comprised some one thousand square miles—plus thirty-six more if we add in the island of Salamis, which was also under Athenian control at this time. Along with its rival Sparta, Athens was exceptional in controlling so large a land mass. However, its territory was smaller than that of Rhode Island, the smallest American state, which is just over twelve hundred square miles. In 480 Athens's population, including slaves, probably amounted to about 150,000, of whom only about 30,000 were adult male citizens.[16] Women had no political and little legal identity. Even so, they were perhaps marginally more prominent than women in Persia—at least if art is any measure of prominence. Not a single sculpted figure of a woman has survived from Persepolis, though royal women did own estates.[17]

Every Athenian citizen was required to serve in the military, though a significant proportion of the thirty thousand would have been seniors and therefore unfit for active combat. Also serving were resident aliens, known as *metoikoi,* who inhabited Attica. The total number of people living on the mainland at the time of the Greco-Persian Wars was probably close to 2 million.

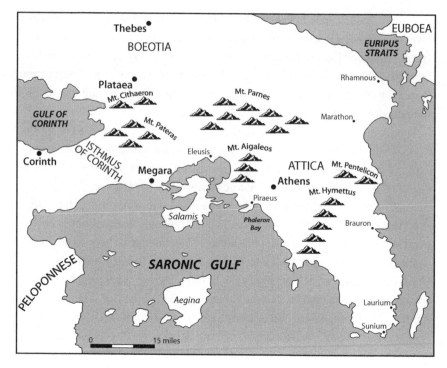

Attica and Environs

Perhaps as many as half of these were slaves. That would certainly have been true for Attica.

There are striking contrasts that pertain particularly to Athens and Persia. The Persians were ruled by an autocratic monarch with the power of life and death over his subjects. There is no evidence that the ethnic Persians enjoyed any form of popular representation, though some Greek cities in their empire had democratic institutions. Athens, however, was committed to the revolutionary principle that decisions had to be based on the will of the majority and that all citizens were equally qualified in determining the direction of public policy. The most important step along the road to democracy had been taken a generation earlier in 508/7, when an aristocrat named Cleisthenes had divided the citizen body into ten tribes, perhaps to destroy the regional power bases of his fellow aristocrats. The roots of Greek democracy are much older, however, and are already detectable in the Homeric poems, dated 725–700 BCE. Athenian democracy would continue to evolve after the Greco-Persian Wars, but by 480 the confidence that it invested in the ordinary, unqualified, and inexperienced adult male was without precedent in human history.

But though every Athenian citizen had the right to express his opinion on any subject under discussion and though every decision depended on the will of the people—that is, the *dēmos*, hence our word "democracy"—those whose opinions carried most influence in the Assembly were predominantly wellborn. A notable exception is the nonaristocrat Themistocles, whose family in Plutarch's words "was too low-born to advance his reputation" and yet whose leadership was critical in this period.[18] It has been estimated that no more than twenty citizens were responsible for policy initiatives at any one time.

Every Athenian had the right, or rather the obligation, to hold public office and to serve as a juror in the court of appeal. Magistrates and all other lesser officials were appointed by lot. Allotment signified that the choice of an appointee was decided by the gods. Only generals, known as *stratēgoi*, and financial officials, such as the treasurers of Athena, were elected by a popular vote. All officials had to undergo scrutiny before taking office, and all had their records examined when their period of office came to an end. Though Athens was a literate society, it also placed much emphasis on oral expression, not only in public but also in private life, in part through the institution known as the symposium, which was especially popular among the elite, where the ability to be informed, articulate, and persuasive was all-important.[19]

The Athenians saw themselves as diametrically opposed to the Persians in part because they had set out on the path to radical, participatory democracy (very different from modern, Western-style representative democracy), whereas the ethnic Persians, like their subjugated peoples, were subject to the rule of one man. They also contrasted their manliness with Persian effeminacy and in other ways judged themselves to be a superior culture. But though the Athenians may have held this viewpoint at the outbreak of the Persian Wars, almost all the evidence for it postdates their victory.

Athenian aristocrats had been visiting Persia from the middle of the sixth century onward, and many may even have been favorably disposed toward its royal house. The ancient world was interconnected through ties of hospitality, specifically on the Greek side through the institution known as *xenia*, a term loosely translated as guest friendship, which placed both guest and host under a reciprocal obligation. *Xenia* served the needs of mobile aristocrats, binding both Greeks and non-Greeks together. Some Athenian aristocrats may have felt a conflict of loyalties at the outbreak of the Greco-Persian Wars, especially those who regarded democracy with suspicion, of whom there was a fair number. Indeed, a few sought refuge with the Persians and supported them in the upcoming war. Despite all the differences, therefore, there was no "political and linguistic iron curtain between Greeks and Persians in Asia," as David Lewis has observed, and it may be that links between ethnic Persians and Athenians were particularly close.[20]

It's impossible to tell the story of Athens from June 480 to August 479 without introducing the Spartans. Sparta, uniquely among Greek city-states, placed overwhelming emphasis upon its military. It was able to do so because its citizens, known as *homoioi* (literally "those who are similar"), were supported by the labors of a subjugated Greek people known as the helots, who worked their masters' estates and who outnumbered the *homoioi* by perhaps as much as seven or eight to one.[21] In consequence, the Spartiates, as they were called, were "the most free of the Greeks and the helots the most enslaved."[22] The *homoioi*, of whom there were about eight thousand in 480, could devote all their time to military training. The joke was that the Spartans got a break from training only when they went to war.

This had both benefits and drawbacks. Sparta came to dominate the Peloponnese but at the expense of its own material culture, which became austere. As a result, Sparta has left us very little architecture except for the remains of houses. We have not much literature, only a few sculptures, and a handful of painted pots, ivories, and terracotta painted masks, though we should bear in mind that the Spartans may well have had a rich song and dance culture, of which little trace now remains.

Persia and Sparta first came into contact with each other around 546 when the Greeks who occupied islands in the eastern Aegean and cities along the now Turkish coastline sent the Spartans a request for military aid against the Persians. The Spartans rejected the request and soon afterward Ionia, as we call this part of eastern Greece, namely Aeolis and southwest Asia Minor, was conquered. But they allegedly sent an embassy to Cyrus the Great warning him "not to commit any act of wanton aggression against any Greek *polis*, since we will not ignore it." When he heard this, Cyrus reputedly inquired, "Who among the Greeks are these Spartans and how numerous are they that they should talk to me like that?"[23]

The Burning of Sardis

Athens's first encounter with Persia occurred in 507 when the *dēmos* sent an embassy to Artaphernes, satrap of Sardis, requesting that they form an alliance

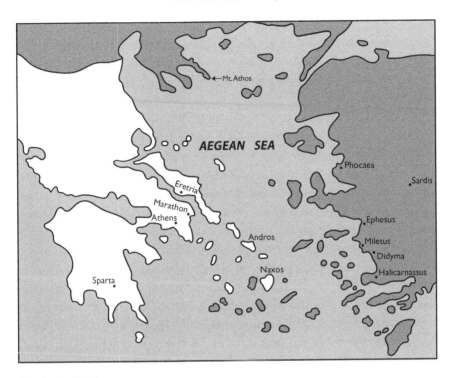

The Ionian Revolt

together against Sparta. Artaphernes, who was apparently as ignorant as Cyrus, inquired of the ambassadors, "Who are the Athenians and where do these people live who are requesting an alliance with the Persians?"[24] He then demanded earth and water, traditional tokens of submission, as the cost of his consenting to an alliance. The envoys agreed, but the citizen body later refused to comply, and nothing came of it.

In 499 the Athenians took a decision that set them on a collision course with Persia. It resulted from a visit by Aristagoras, deputy tyrant of Miletus, a Greek city on today's Turkish coast. Aristagoras was seeking support for the Ionian Greeks and others who wanted to revolt against Persian rule. They had been subjects for nearly half a century, though this had not been wholly to their disadvantage. Indeed, some had prospered, as archaeological and textual evidence indicate.[25] Aristagoras first visited Sparta, where he was rebuffed. The Spartans were never eager to campaign across the sea far from home because of their fear that their helots would revolt in their absence. He then appealed to the Athenians, who agreed to send twenty ships, thereby prompting Herodotus, who thought that this was a very stupid decision, to observe, "It seems easier to deceive a bunch of people than just one man."[26] The Athenians regarded themselves as Ionians so they identified with the Ionian cause.

Perhaps more significantly, however, they were still smarting from the fact that in 504 or thereabouts the Persian satrap Artaphernes had peremptorily ordered them to reinstate Hippias, a hated tyrant who had been expelled in 510 after a Spartan invasion—adding menacingly, "if they wished to stay out of trouble." The Athenians had refused and, by this action, as Herodotus reports, "had openly declared themselves to be enemies of Persia."[27] To exert their influence over a Greek *polis*, the Persians would occasionally set up a local tyrant as their vassal. So the reinstatement of Hippias would, the Persians hoped, bring Athens not only within their sphere of influence but also under their heel. Moreover, it was after the expulsion of Hippias that the Athenians had taken a major step toward becoming a democracy. They deeply resented interference by an imperial power in support of the enemy of their democracy. They had only a small fleet at the time, so twenty ships represented a sizable commitment. Aristagoras also appealed to Eretria, a *polis* on the west coast of Euboea, the island that extends along most of east Attica, and persuaded its people to furnish five ships.

So in 499 the combined naval force of the Athenians and Eretrians sailed across the Aegean and disembarked at Ephesus, thirty miles to the north of Miletus, where they joined the Ionian rebels. They then marched eighty miles northeast to Sardis. Sardis had previously been the main city of the kingdom of Lydia. Under Persian rule since circa 545, it had become the headquarters of the principal Persian satrapy and the center of Achaemenid control in modern-day western Turkey.

Upon arrival the Greeks launched a surprise attack. Artaphernes, who happened to be in Sardis at the time, hastily withdrew to its acropolis, which his men successfully defended. The Greeks captured the rest of the city, but during the fighting some houses caught fire. The fire spread to the Temple of Cybele, the patron goddess of Sardis, also known as the Great Mother, which went up in flames. Because the roofs of houses were mainly made out of straw, the fire spread rapidly and, with no means to control it, consumed everything in its path. It is entirely possible that this catastrophe was unintentional, but the Persians interpreted the destruction of the temple as a deliberate act, for which they held the Athenians and Eretrians chiefly responsible. The Persians may have consecrated an altar outside the temple. If so, they would have regarded its destruction as an affront to their own religious sensibilities.

The Greek forces now withdrew to Ephesus. They had no interest in challenging the enemy on home turf. The Persians pursued them and inflicted a severe defeat, whereupon the Greeks disbanded, each contingent returning to its own city. The Athenians and the Eretrians sailed home. And that was essentially that. The mainland Greeks took no further part in the revolt they had helped to initiate, despite the fact that Aristagoras sent several more appeals for assistance. They simply abandoned the Ionians to their fate.[28] Then in 494 the Persians sacked Miletus, which had instigated the Ionian Revolt. After killing all the soldiers, they enslaved and exiled the rest of the population—a common practice after a siege. This action sent shock waves throughout the Greek-speaking world. Miletus had been the largest and wealthiest of the Ionian cities, and a center of scientific and philosophical inquiry. The Persians went on to plunder the nearby Temple of Apollo at Didyma. As Herodotus tells us, they later "used the burning of the Temple of Cybele as a justification for destroying the holy places of the Greeks."[29] Once Miletus had been sacked, the back of the revolt was broken. With hindsight we can see that it had been doomed from the start.

Did the Athenians feel just a twinge of guilt when Miletus fell? Certainly they should have, even though guilt didn't feature prominently on their emotional radar. But when the Athenian dramatist Phrynichus staged a tragedy entitled the *Capture of Miletus* soon after the destruction of the city, in 493 or 492, it so distressed the Athenians in his audience that they fined him one thousand drachmas "for reminding them of their own troubles," as Herodotus puts it.[30] The words "their own" are highly significant. They indicate that the Athenians took Miletus's fate personally.

The Ionian Revolt was the first major conflict between the Greeks and the Persians—the opening act, in other words, of the Greco-Persian Wars. Though they did not know it at the time, the Athenians would come perilously close to sharing an identical fate to the Milesians.

Darius's Attempted Act of Revenge

Herodotus claims that when King Darius learned that Sardis had been burned down, he did what Cyrus and Artaphernes had done before him, and asked who the Athenians were. It's obvious by now that this is a literary trope, perhaps intended to indicate ill-judged Persian contempt for the Greeks. Learning of their identity, Darius supposedly shot an arrow in the air and said, "O Zeus, may it be granted that I have my revenge upon the Athenians." (Herodotus gives no explanation as to why Darius should invoke a Greek god.) He then ordered a servant to say to him three times whenever he was about to eat dinner each day, "Sire, remember the Athenians."[31] There is a nice irony in this, because in time, of course, the Persians would have reason to wish they could forget the Athenians. The anecdote suggests that the Athenians were on Darius's back burner. They weren't a pressing and urgent concern, merely one to be attended to eventually. Although this makes a good story, it is hardly likely that the king would leave unpunished a dangerous enemy who had raided his territory and supported insurrection.

After the revolt had been crushed, Darius sent envoys to the cities of mainland Greece asking for earth and water. Many states complied, but the Athenians and Spartans threw the envoys into a pit and a well, respectively—an act of sacrilege. In 492 Darius dispatched an expedition to Greece in order to punish Athens and Eretria, but it had to be abandoned because the land force met with strong resistance from Thracians and the fleet was wrecked in a storm off Mount Athos in northern Greece. Two years later he sent another expedition under the joint command of his nephew Artaphernes (namesake and son of the satrap of Lydia) and an experienced general called Datis, who was a Mede.

After sacking Naxos and subjugating other islands in the Cyclades, the expeditionary force assaulted Eretria on the southern coast of Euboea. Its population held out for a week until two rich Eretrians turned traitor—a common practice among aristocrats in the Greek world when things got tough. The Persians "sacked the city and destroyed the sanctuaries, exacting vengeance for the sanctuaries that had been burned down in Sardis," as Herodotus tells us.[32] Very likely this included the Temple of Apollo Daphnephoros (Bearer of Bay), judged to have been one of the most important temples in Eretria.

We might expect the Persians to have implemented the procedure known in Greek as *andrapodismos*; that is to say, the execution of those of fighting age and the selling into slavery of the women and children, as in the case of the Milesians. Herodotus makes no mention of this, however.[33] Instead he tells us that Darius had previously ordered his men to deport the survivors to Susa in the eastern part of his empire. Even so, some either escaped or, less likely, were permitted to remain. We know this because the Eretrians were able to supply seven ships to fight at Artemisium and Salamis a decade later, and because they also provided a contingent of hoplites at Plataea.[34] Presumably those who survived the sack interred the broken sculptures in honor of their gods in their ruined sanctuaries, just as the Athenians would do when the Persians destroyed their sanctuaries a decade or so later.[35]

The Persians then crossed to the Bay of Marathon on the northeast coast of Attica, intending to hand out the same treatment to the Athenians. They chose this spot to land because the exiled tyrant Hippias, who was with them, thought he could count on support from the local aristocracy. Divisions within individual Greek city-states were often so intense that those who had been ousted from power and sent into exile would make common cause with the enemy. No support proved forthcoming, however, and there on the plain of Marathon, with the aid of one thousand Plataeans and an unknown number of slaves, the Athenians defeated the Persians.[36] It was a stunning victory. Herodotus tells us that the Athenians, who were clad in hoplite armor, advanced "at a run." The hoplite carried a spear, a sword, and a concave round shield. He wore a helmet, a corselet made of bronze or leather, and perhaps greaves. Given the fact that the weight of his armor amounted to thirty-five pounds or more, the Athenians' charge was a highly impressive feat. However, some hoplites may have dispensed with their corselets and greaves to speed their advance, thereby reducing the weight they carried to seventeen pounds.[37]

After the battle the Persians returned to their ships and hastily embarked, and the Athenians immediately marched back to Athens. They arrived just in time to prevent the Persians from landing in the Bay of Phaleron, some three miles southeast of Athens, from which they had intended to make an assault on the city. The bay served as Athens's principal roadstead before the development of the Piraeus. Had the Athenians not been at hand to resist them, the Persians would have easily captured the city and set fire to it. The enslaved civilian population would doubtless have been dealt the same fate as the Eretrians and shipped off to Persia.

Herodotus alleges that when the Athenians returned to the battlefield, they counted 192 of their own dead and 6,400 Persians. This is probably a very rough estimate of the Persian dead, but it had certainly been a rout, though some scholars even go so far as to question whether the Persian army was even equal in size to that of the Athenians and Plataeans.[38]

The Spartans, whose help had been requested, arrived soon afterward. They complimented the Athenians on a good day's work and returned home. They had been delayed by a festival and set out for Marathon only after the celebrations had ended. This seems like a pretty feeble excuse, but it has some merit. The Greeks treated religious festivals very seriously. The ex-tyrant Hippias died on the voyage back.

The Athenians commemorated the 192 dead by burying their cremated remains where the men had fallen, heaping up a mound forty feet high.[39] They also set up a cenotaph in the center of Athens, as we know from an inscription that has recently come to light.[40] The Persian dead were treated more cursorily. According to Pausanias, travel writer of the late second century CE, the Athenians falsely claimed that they buried the Persian dead in accordance with divine law, but in reality they "carried the bodies to a trench and tossed them in anyhow."[41] His report was confirmed by a nineteenth-century German topographer, who discovered human remains scattered at the north end of the plain of Marathon. A burial mound near the museum at modern-day Vrana, situated a short distance from the battleground, may mark the grave of the Plataeans who fought alongside the Athenians. This incidentally was the first time that the Athenians had relied on the assistance of slaves in battle. Though Pausanias claims that the Athenians granted them burial, their remains have never been discovered.[42]

Xerxes' Preparations

Herodotus says that when Darius received report of the battle, he became "even more enraged at the Athenians than he had been before and all the more determined to make war on mainland Greece."[43] Either he or his source is probably drawing an inference. We don't know how the king received the news, but it's possible that he wasn't unduly troubled. "Even more enraged" indicates that he was already fired up against the Greeks before he decided to launch his attack on Eretria and Athens. Perhaps he was hoping to soften up the Greeks in preparation for a much larger expedition. He had sent an expedition to northern Greece two years earlier that had met with some success.

Darius died in late 486 and was succeeded by his son Xerxes, "the Great King, King of Kings, King of countries containing all kinds of men, King on this great earth far and wide, son of Darius the King, an Achaemenid, a Persian, son of a Persian, an Aryan, having Aryan heritage," as he styled himself.[44] The Greeks styled him simply "the King," as they did all Persian royalty. It was a compliment of sorts. Xerxes was in his thirties. He was not Darius's oldest son, but his mother was Atossa, daughter of Cyrus the Great, whereas his older brother's mother was a commoner—hence his elevation to the throne.

Like his father, Xerxes may have decided that he couldn't leave the Athenians to gloat over their victory, though it is interesting to note that Herodotus suggests he was initially reluctant to invade Greece and did so partly at the prompting of his cousin and brother-in-law Mardonius.[45] He had other reasons for attacking Greece, however. Herodotus has him claim that in punishing the Athenians he would be securing the boundaries of his empire. He would also be performing an act of filial duty. In the inscriptions that he ordered to be carved throughout his empire, Xerxes stresses the fact that his father had recognized in him the qualities of kingship. What better way to prove this to his people than by finishing off what his father had begun? In Aeschylus's *Persians*, Xerxes' mother Atossa suggests that he undertook the expedition to dispel the widespread rumor, perpetrated by "wicked men"—possibly Greek exiles—that he was a coward and didn't have it in him to be a great warrior like his father.[46] That is pure supposition.

It's also possible that Xerxes wanted to expand the empire, and, if so, westwards was the only way he could go.[47] H. T. Wallinga suggests that the Persians were motivated in large part by Athens's decision to convert itself into a naval power and that they "considered the hugely increased naval potential on their western flank enough threat to be thoroughly perturbed."[48] Perhaps. One thing is clear. The campaign mattered greatly to Xerxes. Though the expedition gave him the opportunity to display his qualities as a military leader, had it been of lesser importance, he might have assigned the task to one of his generals, as his predecessor had done. It is also highly doubtful that he would have left the rest of Greece alone, once he had sacked Athens.[49] He knew he would be gone for several months, even if he secured a quick victory. In the event he was away for the better part of a year.

Xerxes' first task on ascending the throne was to crush a revolt in Egypt, one of the wealthiest of the satrapies. In 484 the satrapy of Babylonia also revolted. It wasn't until the beginning of the following year that he was able to direct his energies and resources into preparing for the invasion of Greece—some three years prior to his departure.[50] Having successfully put down both insurrections, he could take comfort in the fact that he had an army that was well tested in battle. So he had reason to be confident, perhaps overconfident, in the assessment of his prospects. It was that overconfidence—*hubris*, to give it its Greek name—that would bring about his downfall. Such at least was the verdict of Herodotus, who puts the following words into the mouth of Xerxes when he is addressing a special assembly of Persian aristocrats: "If we subdue the Athenians and their neighbors . . . we will demonstrate that the land of Persia shares a border with the realm of Zeus. For the sun will not look down on any land that shares borders with ours because I, with your support, will make all their lands one country, once I have passed through Europe." It is a boast that, in the words of Donald Lateiner, manages "to show insolence to Zeus, the sun, the sky above, and land and sea, as well as towards his fellow men."[51] Whether Xerxes actually delivered such a speech, and whether he was chronically insolent toward the gods as our Greek sources imply, is another matter altogether.

There are obvious reasons for suspecting this to be mere Greek propaganda, added to which the charge of *hubris* or "insolence" can be leveled at virtually any general whose intentions fail in the execution.

The expedition was perhaps the biggest operation that Persia had ever undertaken.[52] Herodotus puts the total number of troops who were drafted at 2,617,610, to whom should presumably be added the usual assortment of camp followers. Most scholars think this figure is wildly exaggerated. A more likely estimate is between 50,000 and 100,000, with 10,000 cavalry.[53] It would have taken a great deal of advance planning to feed even an army of that reduced size on a journey that was going to last at least three months, as well as to provision all the baggage animals and horses. Before setting out, Xerxes established supply depots along the route he intended to take, especially in Thrace and Macedonia. Provisions were conveyed thither "on board merchantmen and ferries from all over Asia."[54] It is clear that Xerxes gathered as much information about the topography of Greece as he could before setting out.

Herodotus claims that Xerxes "searched all the land of the continent" to muster his army.[55] There were twenty-nine contingents representing forty-three ethnic groups, commanded by six generals.[56] In other words, this was a truly multiethnic force, with contributions from peoples living in India, the former Soviet Union, Arabia, Egypt, Turkey, Lebanon, and elsewhere, as well as a large number of Ionian Greeks. It is likely, however, that the core of his army comprised Persians and Medes, since these were the best-trained fighters.[57] It may have been the first time in human history when large numbers of people from different places and ethnicities had encountered one another on a daily basis, learned about each other's customs, and tried to communicate with one another in their various different languages. Oddly, Herodotus never mentions the more exotic peoples in his descriptions of battle, and some scholars believe he adds them merely to point out the diversity of the Persian Empire, since most of the troops that he refers to in combat context—Elamites, Medes, Persians, and Saka—derive from the empire's core regions. The infantry was armed with swords and spears, as well as bows, and wore scaled armor—much lighter than that worn by the Greeks—and carried wicker shields. The Persian cavalry, an elite force, was efficient and highly trained. The men wore metal breastplates and helmets, and their horses may have been armed as well. As it turned out, however, they would play no significant part in the encounter to come.

Herodotus tells us that the total number of warships in Xerxes' fleet when it left Doriscus in Thrace was 1,207. According to H. T. Wallinga, this is plausible "if we assume that all of the ships had only skeleton crews to begin with, i.e. 50 or 60 rowers," to be supplemented by volunteers and conscripts along the way. However, Michael Flower raises the possibility that the fleet numbered only between three hundred and four hundred triremes—the same size in fact as the Greek fleet that fought at Salamis.[58] Like the army, it consisted mainly of Persian subjects—principally Phoenicians, Cypriots, and Ionian Greeks. Very few ethnic Persians served as rowers because they considered rowing a demeaning activity.

What proportion of the empire's manpower was conscripted into the army and navy? A sizable percentage of the workforce had to remain behind to till the land and protect the empire from incursions or insurgency. Probably each satrapy was given a quota of soldiers it was required to provide, and then the decision was taken at the local level as to who should be enlisted. Herodotus tells the chilling story of a wealthy Lydian called Pythius, the grandson of King Croesus, whose five sons had all been drafted into the army.[59] After hosting Xerxes and his entire army—a mammoth undertaking—Pythius, having secured a promise from the king that he would grant any favor he requested, was emboldened to ask if he would release his oldest son from military service so that he would have someone to look after him in old age. Xerxes was incandescent with rage. He had his men slice Pythius's son in two and place the two halves of his body on either side of the road. He then ordered his army to march between them. The anecdote is clearly intended to demonstrate that even those who did the Persian king a signal favor were mere slaves in his eyes; that no one, no matter how closely connected to him, could expect to be excused from military service; and that the king's word was not to be trusted. It is more than likely that this anecdote is an invention either of Herodotus or of his sources, intended to underscore Xerxes' unpredictability and irascibility.[60] What increases the likelihood of this is that we have evidence that the Persians did occasionally permit substitutions when there was a draft.[61]

The Athenians Prepare for Xerxes' Invasion

The Athenians knew that the Persians intended to burn their city to the ground. They'd seen what they'd done already to the Milesians and Eretrians. So they'd worked out long ago that they needed a bold plan of action to have any hope of survival. To their great good fortune, luck had played into their hands. In 483/2, the very same year that Xerxes had begun preparing his invasion, they'd made a silver strike at Laurium in south Attica, extracting the metal from silver-bearing lead ores. It was the politician and general Themistocles, son of Neocles, who bullied, coaxed, cajoled, and inspired the *dēmos* to forsake the pleasure of the moment and devote the wealth it had accrued from the strike to build a fleet. He did so, we can imagine, against powerful opposition.

The decision to convert Athens into a naval power had profound political implications. As Plutarch accurately points out, "Themistocles increased the power of the *dēmos* at the expense of the aristocracy and filled it with boldness, since political influence now passed into the hands of sailors, boatswains, and pilots."[62] This was because the overwhelming majority of the citizen rowers in the fleet belonged to the lowest property-owning group known as the *thētes*, upon which the state now became dependent for its welfare and survival. Metics (resident aliens) and slaves may also have served. The decision to build a fleet also meant that its heavily armed hoplite infantry now had to train as rowers.

Themistocles was in his early forties at the time of the invasion and will be a major figure in our narrative. He is one of very few Greeks of whom we have an intended likeness, a "portrait," though all we possess is a copy made in Roman times. The copy, which is inscribed with his name, was found near the port of Ostia on the Tiber River, close to Rome, in 1939. Though the original may well have been carved in his lifetime, we can't know how accurate a likeness it is. The Greeks, unlike the Romans, never developed a genre of fully individualized portrait sculpture. Instead they favored what is known as "role portraiture," in which they sought to convey ideal types. In the case of Themistocles, the sculptor has adapted the type of the hero Heracles to make the politician and general look heroic. This fact notwithstanding, the head is remarkable for both its intensity and force of character.[63]

From July 483 onward the Athenians applied themselves to the task of increasing the size of their fleet, which probably numbered about fifty triremes at this time. The trireme (literally, a "three-oarer") had been invented either by the Egyptians or by the Phoenicians. It was so named because its rowers sat in banks of three, one above another. The design developed from a warship known as the penteconter, which had a single row of twenty-five oars on each side (*pentekonta* is the Greek for "fifty"). The trireme became the dominant warship in the eastern Mediterranean from the beginning of the fifth century onward, though it didn't compose the whole of the Athenian fleet. Its top speed was about nine knots. It was fitted with a two-pronged bronze ram. The preferred method of attack was to come at the enemy ship astern and rupture its hull along its full length. From modern trials conducted with a reconstructed trireme known as the *Olympias*, we know that a trireme could execute a 180-degree turn in just one minute. Its complement consisted of 170 rowers on benches, along with an assortment of 30 marines and archers, plus the helmsman, all of whom sat, or perhaps in some cases crouched, on the deck.

The decision to turn Athens into a naval power profoundly affected the lives, and perhaps in some cases the mindsets, of virtually everyone residing in Attica—men as well as women, citizens as well as resident aliens, slave as well as free. Rowing alongside 169 others is a highly skilled activity that requires a great deal of practice, and practice takes time. The rowers had to learn how to perform complicated nautical maneuvers, which they had to execute in the heat and din of battle. The helmsman of the *Olympias* had to resort to loudspeakers to communicate with the rowers because "the length of the hull . . . and 170 human sound-absorbing bodies . . . meant that calls at maximum volume reached at most one third of the way down the ship."[64] How, one wonders, did a helmsman communicate to his crew in antiquity? By means of trumpet blasts? By signals passed to other signalers below deck? Incidentally, it's unlikely that naval personnel were required to learn how to swim, even though Herodotus tells us that few Greeks drowned at the Battle of Salamis. The main reason for this was probably because triremes swamp rather than sink, which meant the sailors could cling to the wreckage.

Athens's manpower had to be in intensive training for the summer months from 482 to 480, although many men had to return to their farms to do the plowing, sowing, and harvesting. As there were only thirty thousand citizens, and as many of them were unfit for the rigors of rowing, the state had to conscript noncitizens, the long-term residents known as metics, in order to reach the grand total of forty thousand that was needed to man a fleet of two hundred triremes. Slaves, too, were pressed into service, rowing alongside citizens, possibly even on the same bench. Presumably barracks or tents were provided for all the naval personnel, including those engaged in shipbuilding, both in Phaleron Bay and in the port of Piraeus, which was first developed in the 490s, allegedly on Themistocles' initiative.[65] Families were temporarily split up, wives and children being left to fend for themselves.

The Athenians must have been launching about five or six triremes per month in the three-year period leading up to the Persian invasion to make up the total. Much of the workforce was probably servile, though some of the more skilled craftsmen were probably citizens and metics. Even though the slaves toiling in the shipbuilding yards were probably working a fourteen-hour shift, that was far preferable to laboring in the silver mines or in the quarries, where conditions were extremely hazardous. It was essential that those who built the triremes also served on them, because this way they knew how to repair them when they were damaged. Athens's forests could not possibly have provided sufficient timber for the building of a fleet. So much of the timber had to be imported from Macedon, a major exporter, with which Athens now formed close economic ties. The result of this supreme effort, which, in addition to the construction of the ships, required about forty thousand naval personnel to become skilled in the techniques of naval warfare, was that by the summer of 480—less than three years in total—the Athenians had achieved their objective. They had by far the largest navy in all of Greece. Such a momentous redirection of human and physical resources is virtually unparalleled in the history of human conflict. The downside was that they were now extremely vulnerable to invasion.

Xerxes Prepares to Depart

Xerxes not only had to muster his huge army. He also needed to mobilize a large work team numbering in the thousands, if not the tens of thousands, to enable the amphibious expedition to proceed as smoothly as possible.

To that end he ordered his engineers to build two pontoon bridges across the Hellespont, so that his entire army could cross from Asia into Europe on dry land, so to speak, just as his father Darius had bridged the Hellespont before invading Scythia about thirty years earlier. The Hellespont, which we call the Dardanelles, is the long strip of water that separates modern-day Europe from Asia. It is a particularly treacherous stretch, due both to opposing currents, one on the surface, the other below, and to violent winds from both the Black Sea and the Aegean. The bridges extended from the town of Abydos on Asiatic soil to the coast opposite, a distance of more than two thousand yards. They were made of 674 ships tied together with ropes and anchored parallel to the current. Wicker screens were erected on both sides and earth scattered over planks laid crosswise so that the horses and pack animals would not see the water and panic.[66]

Another engineering feat undertaken by Xerxes' engineers was the cutting of a canal about twenty-four hundred yards in length and nearly sixty-five yards wide through the neck of the most eastern of the three peninsulas at Athos in Chalcidice in northern Greece. Its purpose was to spare his fleet the necessity of circumnavigating the dangerous cape where his father's fleet had foundered two years before the Battle of Marathon. The project, undertaken by local conscripts and army units, took over two years to complete.[67] Modern scholars, like the ancient Romans before them, have cast doubts upon the claim that he actually built the canal, but traces of it were discovered by a British and Greek archaeological team in 2001. He also built a bridge to the east of Chalcidice over the River Strymon, which runs between northeastern Greece and Bulgaria.

From the perspective of the Greeks, it was as if Xerxes wanted to subdue the elements by making war against natural as well as human enemies. That is what he is alleged to have tried to do quite literally when, as Herodotus reports, he ordered that the Hellespont be given three hundred lashes and branded with red-hot irons after the first two bridges were destroyed in a violent storm—an act of cultural sacrilege since the Greeks regarded the Hellespont as a god.[68] Herodotus claims that he also executed the engineers who had been in charge of the construction work for their inferior workmanship—an interesting example of belief in double causation.[69] It is likely, however, that this picture of Xerxes' towering and insensate rage is the product either of Greek propaganda or of the historian's imagination. Herodotus does not tell us when the first bridges were destroyed or how long it took to build their replacement, but it must have been several days, during which the expedition is likely to have been hard pressed for food and water, as well as for fodder for the animals.[70]

Though these projects were intended in part to demonstrate Xerxes' mastery of the elements, they also had a practical application. Xerxes, it has been suggested, was thinking long-term. Once he had conquered mainland Greece, he would need to incorporate the region into the highly effective Persian communications network. The bridges and the canal would help to achieve this objective. We should note, however, that the bridges required constant upkeep, since ancient ships started to rot if kept permanently in the water. Both engineering feats took two to three years to accomplish.

Xerxes mustered his army in eastern Cappadocia at a place of unknown location called Critalla. We don't know what route he took to Sardis. Most scholars assume he followed the Royal Road, the highway that extends from Susa to Sardis, a distance of nearly seventeen hundred miles, which Darius had built. If he did, he must have occasionally taken another route, because Herodotus tells us he passed through a Phrygian town called Kelainai, which lies to the south of the Royal Road.[71] Perhaps he detoured to gather provisions.

The march was an impressive spectacle. After the baggage carriers, the beasts of burden, and a "mixed assortment of troops" came one thousand elite Persian cavalry followed by an equal number of elite Persian spear bearers. Then, after what Herodotus dubs the sacred chariot of Zeus—either he does not know the name of the Persian deity Ahura-Mazda or more likely he cannot bring himself to utter it—came the king, riding in a chariot drawn by Nisaean horses,

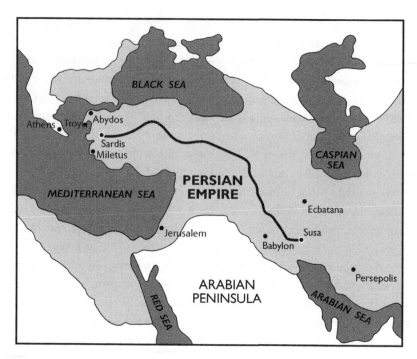

The Royal Road

horses, that is, which were larger than average. An equally long column followed behind. Herodotus tells us that Xerxes got down from his chariot and sought the comfort of a covered wagon "whenever the fancy took him."[72] Bouncing up and down on an uneven surface in a chariot steered by a charioteer who, protocol demanded, was not permitted to ride beside the king but had to march behind him holding the reins must have been a tricky business, and no doubt the fancy took Xerxes whenever the cheering crowds at the side of the road thinned. We may compare Xerxes' progress to that of the British monarch Queen Elizabeth I through her realm. In a similar way, the queen displayed herself to her subjects to create a sense of majesty. For Xerxes it was an opportunity to present himself at the head of a formidable and awe-inspiring army. In the words of Pierre Briant, "To lead his army was to exalt his power as well as to seek to increase it with new conquests that would only impress the subject peoples even more."[73] The drawback was that it slowed his advance considerably.

On arrival at Sardis Xerxes made overtures to prominent Greek exiles, hoping to establish client kingdoms in many Greek cities. He specifically invited those Athenians who were hoping for a restoration of tyranny under Persian rule to accompany him, namely the exiled supporters of the Peisistratid dynasty that produced the tyrant Hippias, since it was his intention to establish a stable, friendly regime in Athens, in much the same way as in 2004 the United States established Hamid Karzai in Afghanistan. The exiled Spartan king Demaratus was also in his entourage, similarly hoping to be reinstated by establishing a government friendly to Persia. Some years before the expedition set out, Demaratus had sent a secret message to the Spartans, warning them of Xerxes' plans. As a result, the Spartans were the first Greeks to learn of the preparations. The exiles no doubt sought to inflame the king with the promise of the enormous wealth that he would acquire from the Greeks consequent upon his victory.[74]

In late September or early October Xerxes sent envoys to all the Greeks, with the exception of the Athenians and Spartans, demanding earth and water. He excluded the Athenians and Spartans presumably because of what they had done to the earlier envoys. The first to medize—that is, switch allegiance to the Persians—were the Thessalians, whose most prominent family, the Aleuadae, was already sympathetic to Persia. All the states as far south as the border between Attica and Boeotia went over to the Persian side with the exception of Doris, the island of Euboea, Phocis, Plataea, and Thespiae, though some that medized later reversed their decision.[75]

His army spent the winter in military training at Sardis. Then in the early spring of 480 Xerxes began his march to Athens. As he approached the Hellespont, he took a detour to the ancient ruins of Troy—or to what he thought was Troy, since the site would have been entirely grassed over and he would hardly have been able to make out its walls. Though Herodotus merely states that Xerxes "had a desire to see Troy," his motive for the detour was surely propagandistic.[76]

On arrival "he climbed up to the acropolis, gazed around, and heard the whole story of what happened there." There he sacrificed one thousand oxen to Troy's main deity, whom the Greeks called Athena, and ordered the *magoi* who were accompanying him to pour libations to the heroes such as Hector who had fallen at Troy. This indicated that the war he was undertaking was one of revenge for the sack of Troy, so the act was clearly aimed at Greeks as well as his subjects.[77] It was as if the king was intending to avenge Athena for the sacrilege that the Achaeans had committed during the sack of Troy when they had stolen her cult statue known as the Palladium. Herodotus goes on to inform us that Xerxes' army panicked during the night, which suggests that Athena rejected the offering.

Though there is no reason to doubt the historicity of Xerxes' visit to Troy, Herodotus or his sources may have included this last incident to underscore the doomed nature of the expedition. Xerxes frequently ignored warnings sent by the gods, according to Herodotus's construction of events. He also drew more than once from the legend of the Trojan War to bolster the legitimacy of the invasion. After crossing into Europe, he desecrated the shrine of Protesilaus in Elaeus, Protesilaus being the first Achaean to have set foot on Trojan soil.[78]

Xerxes arrived at Abydos around May and immediately began supervising the crossing of the Hellespont. Herodotus tells us that he reviewed his army seated on a marble throne, flushed with pride and dreams of imperial conquest. He couldn't even see the waters of the Hellespont because of all his ships. The land round about, too, was dense with soldiers, their arms and armor glittering in the sunlight. Xerxes "counted himself blessed"—that's the word Herodotus uses, almost as if there's something spiritual about the sight of his army—"and then burst into tears." Observing his distress, his uncle Artabanus came up to him and asked him why he was weeping. "I was suddenly overcome by pity at the brevity of human life," the king replied. "I was reflecting that not one of these men will be alive in one hundred years' time." He might have said as General Eisenhower did on the morning of D-Day, "It is very difficult to look a soldier in the face knowing you might be sending him to death." It's a moment of intense pathos, but it doesn't last. How could it? Herodotus tells us that Xerxes now watched his men cross "under the lash." In other words, he suggests that he had lost his humanity and reverted to type as an oriental potentate, though, once again, we may strongly suspect that this is either propaganda or Herodotus's imagination at work.

In reality it would have been impossible to conduct an inspection of the entire army at Abydos. The plain isn't big enough. So the episode is probably invented by Herodotus, his intention being to show the reader what any leader would have been thinking at this moment. He tells us that the crossing took seven days and seven nights—an impressive feat.[79] At Doriscus the king counted his troops by the sheep-pen method and then divided them into three columns. After passing through Thrace, he skirted Chalcidice and then turned south into Macedon, his fleet keeping pace with his infantry.

Day after day, led by Greek scouts, the three columns snaked their way toward Athens. What if anything did the non-Greeks in the expeditionary force know about the city they were attacking? Perhaps some of them had encountered Athenian pottery and coinage. But what if anything had they heard about the Battle of Marathon? Though there was talk of plunder, Greece was poor

Greece and the Aegean

compared with Persia. They would be gone at least a year—longer if they were the unlucky ones who were required to stay behind to do garrison service once the main army had withdrawn. Yet the burning down of the Temple of Cybele in Sardis was an act of desecration that had to be avenged. And there was pride in serving in an army drawn from the four corners of the empire. For the first time it was evident to the soldiery how disparate and extensive the empire was.

The progress of the army through Greece was an impressive spectacle, and the memory of it would live on. Herodotus reports that the Thracians "down to my day do not plow up the road that the king marched along with his army or sow any seeds in it, but hold it in profound reverence."[80] Those Greeks who offered hospitality to the king no doubt did so in the hope of securing either a favor or a reward for their pains. The people of Acanthus, a *polis* on the Athos peninsula that was close to the canal that Xerxes had constructed, received a set of Median clothing in exchange for their hospitality.[81] Their response to such bountifulness is not recorded.

As the army advanced, it grew in size as more communities joined the Persian cause, some by compulsion, others voluntarily. Such was the effectiveness of Xerxes' charm offensive and terror tactics that in the conflict to come more Greeks would fight alongside the Persians than against them.[82]

The Athenians Join the Greek Coalition

The news that Xerxes was heading in their direction came as no surprise to the Greeks. His preparations had been widely bruited three years ago or more, and in recent months there must have been talk of little else. In fact, Xerxes calculated it would be greatly to his advantage that the Greeks should hear of the scale of his preparations, since this could be expected to have a distinctly chilling effect upon their spirits. When in December 481 or January 480 he captured some spies who had been sent to Persia to report on his preparations, he did not execute them as might have been expected. Instead he gave them a tour, confident in the knowledge that they would give a detailed report of everything they had seen when they returned home.

So early in the autumn of 481, when the Persian army was preparing to winter at Sardis, representatives of all the Greek states that were determined to oppose the Persians met at Sparta. There they formed a coalition, "agreeing to suspend hostilities and their wars with one another"—a phrase that tells us much about their current state of division.[83] It was fortunate that there was a preexisting loose alliance known as "the Lacedaemonians [i.e., Spartans] and their allies," commonly referred to today as the Peloponnesian League, which provided an embryonic structure around which the new alliance could be formed. Since Sparta was the leader of this league, it was agreed that a Spartan general should have command of the coalition both on land and at sea, despite the fact that it had only a very small fleet. Presumably the allies thrashed out what financial contribution each should make to the cost of transportation, supplies, and so on.[84] They also agreed to send envoys to Corcyra (Corfu), Crete, and Sicily to seek assistance. In the event, their overtures were rebuffed.

It would be fascinating to know how the Athenians came away from this meeting. Given the geographic base of the Peloponnesian League, which comprised by far the majority of the infantry, they knew that the coalition would be reluctant to commit its forces to the defense of northern Greece and therefore couldn't count on their allies for protection. Either now or at a later meeting there was discussion about transferring the naval command to the Athenians given the size of their fleet, but this suggestion was rejected. So the Athenians yielded, in the words of Herodotus, "because they considered the survival of Greece to be of paramount importance and because they realized that, if they all quarreled about the leadership, Greece would be destroyed, and they were right to think this."[85] It might have seemed to be a rare instance of selflessness, but in actuality the Athenians needed the rest of the Greek fleet just as much as it needed them.

Only thirty-one states are known to have joined the alliance—a striking indication both of the disunity of the Greeks and of the fact that not all of them regarded Persia as the enemy, as well as of the extent of Persia's hegemony over the Greek world at this time.[86] Domestic squabbles in some cases took precedence over the common good. Several states remained neutral, waiting on events. The Argives refused to join because of their intense hatred of the Spartans. The Thessalians saw the invasion as an opportunity to take revenge on their longtime enemies, the Phocians. The Aeginetans, by contrast, rose to the occasion and suspended their hostilities with Athens. The names of the allied contingent are preserved on the so-called Serpent Column, which was set up at Delphi once the war had ended. Thebes refused to join the coalition, while Argos openly sided with the Persians.

The allied campaign did not begin auspiciously. Initially the Greeks decided to take a stand at the Vale of Tempe, situated on the border between Macedon to the north and Thessaly to the south, there to await the Persians. They did so in response to a request from the Thessalians to send a force of ten thousand to defend their land. When they got there, however, in May, probably around the time when Xerxes was crossing the Hellespont, they realized that the Persians could simply bypass them by taking one of several different routes south, so they promptly withdrew. This raises serious questions. How could the allies be so ill-informed about basic topography? Didn't they have any clear information about the terrain of Thessaly when they marched north? Had no one in the south any precise knowledge of the north? The allies had had months to work out where it was best to oppose the Persians. Admittedly their intention to hold the line at Tempe was determined by their desire to keep the Thessalians on board, but their ignorance and disorganization seems surprising, if not willful— all the more so since Xerxes had excellent reconnaissance and planned well in advance. Though geographic knowledge was very limited in the ancient world, this in no way excuses the discrepancy in preparation between the Greeks and the Persians.

The Greeks returned to the Isthmus of Corinth, where they had originally mustered. They now decided to dispatch seven thousand infantry to the narrow pass at Thermopylae ("Hot Gates," so named for its hot sulfur springs), situated on the main route from northern to southern Greece, since it "appeared to be narrower than the one that led to Thessaly."[87] Meanwhile they sent their fleet, which comprised 271 triremes, to Cape Artemisium in Euboea, roughly opposite Thermopylae. Even at this point, however, there was talk of retreating to the Isthmus of Corinth without putting up a fight. Since the isthmus lies some forty miles southwest of Attica, this means that the allies were prepared to abandon Athens to its fate without engaging in any hostilities.

-II-

The Evacuation

"Some Better Oracle"

Even before Xerxes set out from Sardis, most realistically minded Athenians must have come to the painful realization that if the allies failed to safeguard northern Greece, there were four options available: the first was to come to terms with the Persians, in effect to medize and accept loss of sovereignty; the second was to risk open battle, hoping against hope for another victory like Marathon, albeit against a much larger expeditionary force; the third was to prepare for a siege, which they could hardly expect to withstand given the inadequacy of their defenses; and the fourth was to evacuate the entire population before the Persians arrived. It was this last option that carried the day. So in order to save the *polis* as an independent political entity, the *dēmos*, that is to say, the Athenian people, would abandon their land to the invader. It was a radical course—as radical as any that the Athenians had taken. The likely outcome, however, was that their homes, temples, and ancestral tombs would be destroyed. The landscape of Attica would never be the same again.

But even though the majority favored this course of action, no doubt a number of die-hards loudly protested that they were not prepared to go down this path. Indeed, we may assume that when evacuation was first suggested, it

The view from Delphi looking south toward the Peloponnese

unleashed a storm of anger among the older, more conservative element and probably, too, among what passed for the religious hardliners who could not tolerate the thought of temples being laid waste. The question to be addressed therefore was: What did the gods advise?

Whenever any momentous decision involving a whole community had to be made, it was customary for Greeks to send representation to an oracular sanctuary. There the god, most typically Apollo or Zeus, or perhaps a hero, spoke through his appointed mouthpiece. There were many such sanctuaries throughout the Greek-speaking world, but none had greater prestige than Delphi, a place full of mystery that nestles within the lower slopes of the Parnassus Mountains just north of the Peloponnese, seventy-five miles northwest of Athens. So probably in the late summer or early fall of 481 the Athenian Assembly voted to send two sacred ambassadors known as *theopropoi* to consult Apollo. There were only nine days during the year when Apollo was available for consultation—one day per month from March/April onward until winter set in—so the *theopropoi* would have had to time their visit to coincide with the god's schedule. (During the three winter months Apollo resided with the fabled Hyperboreans, who, as their name indicates, lived "beyond the North Wind," perhaps in the Black Sea region.) Apollo's mouthpiece was a woman known as the Pythia, so named because she was consecrated to Apollo Pythios, whom she served for life, submitting herself to a strict regimen, which included abstention from sexual intercourse.

Sending ambassadors to Delphi was a high-risk strategy, since in effect it dumped the problem in the god's lap and there was no knowing what he would recommend. I say "recommend" because it was rarely the practice of Apollo to assert unambiguously what course of action to follow. As the Ionian philosopher Heraclitus phrased it, "The lord whose oracle is at Delphi neither conceals nor reveals, but indicates."[1] Consulting the god was, however, a way to achieve political consensus. Indeed, it may have been the last resort in an emergency like this one.

Herodotus provides us with a detailed description of the consultation.[2] He tells us that the *theopropoi* first performed "the customary rituals" in the forecourt of the sanctuary. This would have included bathing in the springs of Delphi as a rite of purification, paying a fee for the purchase of a sacrificial cake, and performing blood sacrifice. In most circumstances petitioners had to wait in line before they could put their questions to the god, so they had to arrive at the sanctuary several days in advance of the appointed consultation day. This was not the case with our *theopropoi,* however, because the temple had been paid for in part by a very wealthy Athenian *genos* or "noble kin-group," known as the Alcmaeonidae. So the Athenians were in the god's good graces and had been awarded *promanteia* or the right of prior consultation—the right, in other words, to skip to the head of the queue of petitioners. The *theopropoi* were escorted into the *megaron* or "great hall," where consultations took place, and sat down.

What exactly did the ambassadors encounter once they entered the *megaron*? The independent historian Tom Holland evocatively describes the scene as follows:[3] "The Pythia, an old woman in a young girl's dress, appeared almost a thing of grotesquerie, ill suited, certainly to be the vessel of golden Apollo. Already, however, as vapors from the cauldron she was perched upon caressed her parted thighs and curled beneath the skirt of her virgin's tunic, she was shuddering with mantic ecstasy: the trance had come upon her." The strong whiff of the erotic, not to say faintly pornographic, suggested by "parted thighs" and "shuddering with mantic ecstasy" are not documented in any ancient source. As for the vapors, the jury is out. Recent research suggests that due to the meeting of geological fault lines at Delphi a buildup of mephitic gases *might* have occurred in the *megaron*. So it is possible, but by no means certain, that the Pythia might at times have been in a trance or some altered state of consciousness induced by these gases, though there would have been considerable fluctuation in the gaseous emissions. In addition, the only literary evidence to support this claim dates to the Roman period. Whatever the truth, however, we need hardly doubt that on entering the sacred space the ambassadors fell victim to a quasi-mystical experience, as their eyes gradually adjusted to the darkness and they dimly took in the figure of the Pythia.[4]

Before they had a chance to put their question to the god, however, the Pythia, whose name was Aristonike, a woman of uncertain age, intoned or perhaps "spewed," to use Holland's colorful verb, a dire prediction. Preempting the petitioner was unusual at an oracular shrine, but not exceptional. According to Sophocles' version of events in *Oedipus the King*, it happened to Oedipus when he went to Thebes to ask who his real parents were.[5] In this case it reflected the urgency of what the god had to say, which Herodotus has preserved in the form of twelve lines of hexameter verse. Though the verses are likely to be an invention of the *prophētai* or interpreters whose purpose was to give meaning to what was incomprehensible to the layperson, they probably capture accurately enough the spirit of Apollo's advice:[6]

> Wretched men, why do you sit here? Fly from the remotest dwellings of your land and the topmost peaks of your wheel-shaped *polis*. For neither its head, nor its body, nor the tips of its toes or fingers remain firm, nor is its middle part left, but all is ruined. A conflagration, in combination with ruthless Ares, who drives a Syrian chariot, brings it to its knees. He will destroy many other fortresses and not only yours. Many temples belonging to the immortals he will give over to devouring fire, ones that now stand dripping with sweat and quaking with fear. From their topmost crest black blood pours, presaging the inevitability of distress. Go forth from this sanctuary and open your heart to evil.

Herodotus states that when the ambassadors heard this, they regarded their situation as "very grave." Rightly so. Athens as a physical entity was going to be wiped off the face of the earth. Not only that, but its temples would be destroyed. The "inevitability of distress" was spelled out in a way that left the Athenians with no alternative. Their only course of action was to migrate, since "many other fortresses" would fall, signifying that the cause of Greece was effectively doomed. They must settle as far away from their homeland as possible, presumably in the West, in either Sicily or southern Italy, already dense with Greek settlements and beyond the reach of the Persians. Resistance was futile. The god offered them nothing. The hopelessness of their predicament could not have been made more clear.

The oracular response should not have taken the *theopropoi* entirely by surprise. Delphi was consistently supportive of the Persian invasion for politically motivated reasons. The oracle had a long-standing relationship with Persia, dating back to the reign of Xerxes' predecessor Darius I. It had earlier condemned Miletus, leader of the Ionian Revolt, as "the instigator of wicked deeds."[7] A Persian takeover of the shrine was almost inevitable, given its extreme vulnerability, and it was important for the standing of the god to be seen supporting the winning side. The priesthood may not have been eager to see the Persians triumph, but most were eager to save their necks as well as their jobs. In short, Delphi saw no alternative but to support the invasion and made pronouncements accordingly.[8]

An interesting question arises as to whether it might have been Xerxes' preference that the Athenians vacate their land for good as the first oracle suggested, rather than suffer the punishment he would otherwise be handing out to them. What Xerxes must have realized before he set out from Persia is that if he could remove the Athenians from the equation, his conquest of mainland Greece was virtually assured.

We don't know how long the envoys hung around outside the sanctum, pondering what to do next. The Pythia had ordered them to leave her sanctuary—an unusual admonition, surely—so it cannot have been very long. No doubt the expressions on their faces said everything to anyone who happened to be watching. And someone was. Herodotus tells us that a certain Timon, son of Androboulos, "a very eminent Delphian," went up to them and advised them to go back inside the sanctum clutching suppliant branches and to request a second oracle. We know nothing else of Timon, but it is not inconceivable that he knew of the Athenian mission in advance. It's even conceivable that he was informed by those Athenians who were determined at all costs to make some sort of stand against the Persians. Quite possibly there was a small Delphic faction that urged resistance to Persia. We know so little about the machinations and internal politics of Delphi that it is impossible to determine what Timon's motivation might have been. What is clear, however, is that he had clout with the priesthood and used his "eminence" to persuade them to allow the *theopropoi* to return.

So the ambassadors plucked up courage and entered the sanctum a second time. They then addressed the god as follows:[9] "Lord Apollo, deliver some better oracle concerning our fatherland and show respect for these suppliant branches which we are bearing as we approach you. If you don't, we will not depart from your holy of holies but remain here till we die." "Some better oracle" seems to make no sense at all. How could Apollo seemingly advise one course of action one moment, and then another the next? How could two quite separate oracles be produced in short succession? Or to put it differently, how could Delphi permit itself to be manipulated by petitioners assuming the role of suppliants? This state of affairs is only comprehensible if, as noted already, we understand an oracle to be something other than a straightforward recommendation. Rather, it was a divine monition that required interpretation in accordance with the prescription that was engraved on the sanctuary's retaining wall: "Know yourself."

There is another oddity. The ritual of supplication was performed most commonly by those who, being in immediate danger, were seeking protection from someone or some group stronger than themselves. The *theopropoi* were not, of course, in any immediate danger themselves. It seems that they assumed the role of suppliants on behalf of their *polis*, with which they now asked to be identified. It was as if Athens itself, its entire people, was seeking asylum.

Herodotus tells us that the god consented to "their prayer." "Threat of desecrating his sanctuary" might be a better way of putting it, since their deaths, presumably by starvation, would pollute the sacred space and compromise its sanctity. This would be all the more offensive in light of the fact that Apollo was the god of purification par excellence. Accordingly, Apollo, speaking again through Aristonike, delivered a second oracle, which Herodotus again reproduces in hexameter verse:[10]

> Pallas Athena cannot propitiate Olympian Zeus, even though she prays with many utterances and profound wisdom. But I will make this pronouncement to you, which I have fixed firm in adamant. When everything else has been captured which the ordinary marker of Cecrops [an early king of Athens] and the summit of divine Cithaeron [a mountain near Thebes] hold between them [meaning all Boeotia and Attica], broad-ruling Zeus shall give a wooden wall to the Thrice-born [i.e., Athena], and it alone shall never be destroyed but shall bless you and your children. Do not peacefully await the cavalry and great army of infantry that is coming from the mainland, but turn your back on it and withdraw [presumably meaning that the Athenians should give up any idea they might have of defending Athens by land]. On a day yet to come you will stand against them. O divine Salamis, you will bring death to the sons of women either when Demeter is scattering [i.e., in spring] or when she is coming together [i.e., in the fall].

It was indeed a better oracle than the first—but only marginally so. The allusion to Athena vainly seeking to propitiate Zeus was perhaps intended to suggest that not all the gods had washed their hands of Athens. Indeed, it may hint at some division within the Delphic priesthood. It can hardly have filled the envoys with joy, but there was nothing else they could do at this point but return to Athens. They had to make the best of a bad job. So they departed, no doubt in haste, though not before copying the oracle down. It was evidently important that they got the wording exactly right.[11]

"The Wooden Wall"

Riding perhaps on horseback, at least where the terrain permitted, the ambassadors probably arrived back in Athens the next day. As soon as they returned, they requested an audience with the Boulē or Council of 500, fifty members of whom were appointed by lot from each of the ten tribes. Each tribal contingent served as *prytaneis* or "presidents" in rotation for thirty-five or thirty-six days, during which period they were fed at public expense. In addition, seventeen members, one-third of the *prytaneis*, were on duty day and night to deal with emergencies. Hearing the envoys' report, those on duty summoned a meeting of the full Council of 500, before whom the ambassadors again recounted their story. The Council then called an extraordinary meeting of the Ekklēsia or Assembly, which all citizens were expected to attend. It is likely, too, that the oracle was referred to the Council of the Areopagus, an aristocratic body numbering about 150, which was regarded as the guardian of the state and which was highly influential in matters to do with religion. The Areopagus (literal meaning "Hill of Ares"), which gave its name to the council, lies a short distance northwest of the Acropolis. The Assembly was probably scheduled for a few days in advance so as to enable those who lived in the outlying demes to make arrangements to attend.

The Assembly met at dawn in a hollowed-out part of a hill known as the Pnyx, which lies about four hundred yards west of the Acropolis. It is reckoned that in the fifth century some six thousand Athenians generally attended—about one in five of the full citizen body. Given the critical nature of the present debate, however, the number on this occasion was probably considerably larger. The debate is likely to have lasted several hours. At no time within living memory had there been more at stake for Athens and its citizenry.

We don't know whether the envoys made mention of the first oracle or whether the Council had taken upon itself to suppress it as being too pessimistic and not in the public interest. Either way, the discussion seems to have focused exclusively on the second oracle and especially on how to interpret the

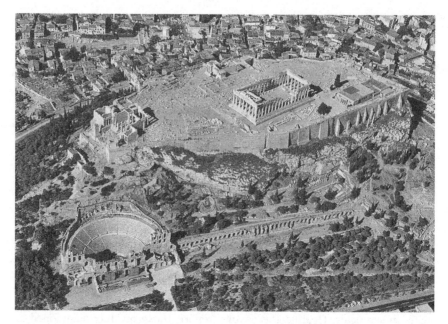

Aerial view of the Acropolis

puzzling phrase "wooden wall."[12] Some of the older citizens, taking this to be
a reference to a thorn hedge that surrounded the Acropolis, augmented perhaps
by a wooden stockade, concluded that the god was prophesying that the Acropolis would survive the coming attack unscathed. Herodotus's account suggests
that the defensive system surrounding the Acropolis was entirely makeshift,
but, as Richard Tomlinson[13] has pointed out, it still possessed its Mycenaean
walls. Others, including the younger citizens, interpreted the wooden wall as a
reference to their fleet, and they now began urging their compatriots "to abandon everything else and get their ships ready."[14]

The final two lines of the second oracle—"O divine Salamis, you will bring
death to women's sons either when Demeter is scattering or when she is
coming together"—were problematic, however. The professional oracle mongers known as *chrēsmologoi*, who gave advice to the Assembly from time to
time in their capacity as experts, interpreted this to mean that the Athenians
would be defeated in a naval battle near Salamis, the largest island in the
Saronic Gulf.

It is now that Themistocles, the politician who had urged the Athenians to
use their silver to build a fleet, enters Herodotus's narrative for the first time.
Themistocles forcefully argued that if the Athenians were going to sustain a

defeat near Salamis, the god would not have described the island as "Divine Salamis" but rather as "Cruel Salamis." Once he had pointed this out, Herodotus continues:[15] "The Athenian *dēmos* decided that his interpretation was superior to that of the oracle mongers, who opposed fighting by sea and were against putting up any resistance at all, and who instead were in favor of abandoning Attica and establishing their homes elsewhere." It is odd that the *chrēsmologoi* were unanimously opposed to armed resistance. Perhaps they were taking their orders from Delphi, which as we saw counseled submission to Persia. We do not know what affiliation there might have been between the oracular seat, its priesthood, and the *chrēsmologoi*, who seemingly operated independently but who were perhaps accountable to Delphi in some undisclosed way.

The result of the debate was that the Athenians "resolved after taking the oracle into account to meet the barbarians who were invading Greece with all their people and their entire naval force, in obedience to the god and with those of the Greeks who wanted to accompany them." The wording of the resolution indicates the degree to which the Assembly judged it essential to be acting in accordance with Apollo's will. Clearly, the *dēmos* did not see itself at complete liberty to determine the best course of action. On the contrary, its decision, ostensibly at least, had to be based as much on the will of Apollo and his interpreters as on military considerations.

It would be fascinating to know how long the debate lasted and what proportion of the *dēmos* eventually voted for the resolution to abandon Attica and fight a naval battle against the Persians. Was there a comfortable majority, or was it a close run thing? As we have noted, there may have been something of a generational divide. It would certainly make sense if the older generation was more reluctant to abandon Attica than the younger generation. Voting in the Assembly wasn't done by counting. That would hardly have been practical at a gathering that numbered several thousands. Instead the decision was reached by a simple show of hands, accompanied no doubt by impassioned shouting on both sides. (Exceptions to voting by a show of hands was the procedure known as ostracism, in which the *ostraka* or potsherds cast against each candidate were counted, and trials by jury, where votes cast as ballots were counted.) It is possible that the poor supported the proposal more vigorously than the wealthy, since they had less to lose by abandoning their homes. Once it had been carried, the motion immediately acquired the force of law, to which every citizen and noncitizen was now indissolubly bound. It then received the designation *psēphisma*, a word that derived from *psēphos*, which means among other things a pebble that is used for counting.

The decision to abandon Attica has been justly praised as "a remarkable example of Athenian democracy in action." And so it was, given the fact that it required the aristocracy to acquiesce in the destruction of its landed estates. Even if the motion was carried comfortably, it can hardly have been unanimous. Yet everybody had to accept the will of the majority. That was how democracy worked. I cannot emphasize too strongly that the implications of the vote were profound, since, if Themistocles and his supporters had lost the debate, Athens might well have ceased to exist, at least in the form in which we know it today. And even if the *dēmos* had managed to make a go of it elsewhere by uprooting itself as the first oracle recommended, it's virtually inconceivable that Athens's great cultural accomplishments of the mid-fifth century would have come into being.

So, yes, to reiterate, this was one of the most significant decisions that the Athenians ever took. And it was all the more momentous, and perhaps all the more traumatic, in light of the fact that as a people they claimed to be autochthonous—sprung from the earth—tracing their descent from Erechtheus, an early king and founder of the *polis*.[16] The story went that Erechtheus had been sired by Hephaestus, whose semen Athena wiped off her thigh with a handful of wool after he had unsuccessfully tried to impregnate her. The goddess then tossed the wool onto the ground, whereupon the semen impregnated Gaia, the personification of the earth, who thus engendered the earthborn Athenian people. The myth was making the argument that the Athenians' attachment to the land of Attica was indissoluble. The fact that the city was named for the goddess no doubt gave it further force in the collective consciousness.

What the Athenians decided at this meeting of their Assembly was, moreover, no less radical for the Greeks as a whole, because, as Herodotus notes, "If the Athenians in dread of the invader had evacuated their land [and founded a new city elsewhere] or if they had not evacuated it but remained there and surrendered to Xerxes, no one would have been able to oppose the king by sea."[17]

The Athenians were not the only people to carry out an evacuation before the arrival of the Persians. According to Diodorus Siculus, writing in the first century BCE, the Plataeans and Thespians, who lived in southern Boeotia, evacuated too, though they chose to take refuge in the Peloponnese.[18] As all the Thespian hoplites had been killed at Thermopylae, only women, children and elderly males would have made the trek. A total evacuation to the Peloponnese on similar lines does not seem to have been an option that the Athenians considered, perhaps because they were far too numerous or because they would not have been welcome.

The Order to Evacuate

Following the vote to abandon Athens and resist the Persians at sea, another decree was passed on a motion proposed by Themistocles that laid down the provisions for the evacuation. There may have been an interval of weeks or even months between the original vote and this new motion so as to enable the details to be worked out. Themistocles brought his proposal before the Assembly for ratification probably in October or November of 481.

Though the original decree does not survive, an inscription whose lettering is of early third-century BCE date cut into a block of Pentelic marble that came to light at Troezen, a small city-state on the northeast coast of the Peloponnese, purports to be a copy of the actual text since it begins with the word *edoxe*, "it seemed good," which is how decrees of the Athenian *dēmos* traditionally began. Whether it is an exact replica of the decree proposed by Themistocles is, however, highly questionable, since some of the terminology it uses is anachronistic.[19] Indeed, George Cawkwell goes so far as to call it "bogus."[20] Its authenticity is further undermined by the fact that it does not seem consistent with the chronology of Athens's plans for evacuation. Andrew Burn, for instance, is of the opinion that the inscription "seems to assemble together resolutions which almost certainly . . . must have been taken at different times."[21]

These problems apart, most scholars would agree that the inscription contains "a historical kernel" and that, irrespective of the extent to which it preserves the text of the original, at the very least it sheds an invaluable light on the way in which the evacuation was imagined to have taken place. The inscription begins as follows:[22] "Gods! It was resolved by the Council and the *dēmos*. Themistocles, son of Neocles of the deme Phrearroi, proposed. The city is to be entrusted to Athena, the protector of Athens, and to all the other gods for them to guard and to defend against the barbarian on the country's behalf." Many must have thought that it was a forlorn hope to trust in the gods, especially in light of the fact that Apollo had told the Athenians that a number of temples were going to be given over to devouring fire. In effect, what this wording probably meant was that the Athenians were undertaking an evacuation. It was, in other words, a face-saving euphemism, alluding only obliquely to the fact that Athens and its temples were going to be abandoned to their fate. The decree continues: "All Athenians and foreigners living in Athens are to settle their wives and children in Troezen. . . . [Elderly people and] possessions are to be deposited on Salamis. The treasurers and the priestesses [are to remain guarding the possessions] of the gods on the Acropolis." Troezen (modern day Trizina), a coastal city some fifty miles to the southwest of Attica by sea, was probably chosen as a place of refuge because it had long-standing connections with Athens, despite being in the Peloponnese. The legendary Athenian hero Theseus was said to have been the son of Aethra, daughter of the Troezenian king Pittheus.

It is highly significant that the decree concerned itself with "foreigners living in Athens." These were long-term residents, known as *metoikoi*, who came to live in Athens mainly because of the commercial opportunities it offered. Metics, at least in the fourth century, had to pay a regular, presumably monthly poll tax, known as the *metoikion*. This amounted to one drachma for an adult male and half a drachma for an adult female living on her own. They were also required to perform military service, either as hoplites or as rowers. We don't know how many metics were resident in Athens in the early fifth century, but there was evidently a sufficient number for the Athenians to be eager to make use of their services as rowers. The directive that metics should settle their wives and children in Troezen indicated that they were being put on an equal footing with citizens. It was also a way of securing their services in the upcoming naval engagement.

Troezen was probably the most favored location for the refugees because it was the most secure. Even if northern Greece fell, the Peloponnesians would hope to hold the line at the Isthmus of Corinth, which lies about fifty-five miles to the north of Troezen. When the Troezenians set up a copy of the decree in the third century BCE, it is likely that they wanted to memorialize the fact that their ancestors had provided refuge for the Athenians—a powerful indication that they took pride in the humanitarianism of their ancestors.

The island of Salamis, which was under Athenian control, was also an obvious destination for the evacuees because of its proximity to Attica, only a third of a mile from the Attic coast at its nearest point. However, its very proximity made it vulnerable, and it was probably for that reason that the decree designated the island as the refuge for Athens's elderly, probably those aged fifty-five and older, not least because the elderly were, to put it bluntly, expendable. According to Herodotus, however, when Themistocles later sought to persuade the Greek coalition to fight at Salamis, he claimed that women and children, rather than the elderly, had been conveyed to the island.[23] If we are to trust Herodotus, it is conceivable that Themistocles did this in order to make his appeal more compelling.

There was a third destination that is not mentioned in the inscription, namely Aegina, an island in the Saronic Gulf approximately thirty-five miles southwest of Athens. Until very recently the Athenians and the Aeginetans had been at war with one another, and this most likely is why the island is not mentioned as a refuge.[24] In fact, a large part of the reason why Athens, in Thucydides' memorable phrase, had decided in 493 to "attach itself to the sea" and convert itself into a maritime power was its fear of Aegina.[25] Perhaps, as Barry Strauss has suggested, the Aeginetans now "wished to make amends for their past."[26] Or perhaps they saw their survival to be dependent on a cessation of hostilities with Athens. The Athenians were in no position to impose, though it may be that the Spartans, who exercised some leverage with the Aeginetans, put pressure on them.[27] Whatever the Aeginetan motive in joining the alliance, it constitutes a remarkable instance of cooperation between two erstwhile bitter foes.

The decree also contained a provision for the recall of men who had been exiled in the 480s: "In order that all the Athenians should be united [literally "of one mind"] in defending themselves against the barbarians, those who have been sent into exile for ten years are to depart for Salamis and wait there until the *dēmos* has decided what to do about them." This was a reference, perhaps primarily, to victims of ostracism, a constitutional safeguard thought to have been introduced circa 508/7 at the prompting of Cleisthenes with the intention of defusing conflict between high-profile political opponents. Once a year the *dēmos* was formally asked if it wished to invoke the process. If it answered in the affirmative, a kind of negative election took place two months later between any number of candidates. If six thousand votes were cast in total (less likely against one candidate), the individual who received the most votes was instructed to leave Athens for ten years. The votes were inscribed on potsherds known as *ostraka*, from which the word "ostracism," *ostrakismos* in Greek, derives.

The provision to recall the exiles raises a number of issues. Clearly it could not be enforced. Compliance depended on the goodwill of the exiles, and some may have been too embittered or too mistrustful to return. There is also the question as to how the invitation—or is it an order?—was to be promulgated. What steps did Athens take to notify the exiles? And once they arrived on Salamis, how long were they expected to "wait" while their fate was being decided? The fact that the *dēmos* had not yet made up its mind what to do with the exiles once they returned perhaps suggests that the merits of each were to be examined on a case-by-case basis, presumably by a formal vote in the Assembly.[28] This can hardly have been reassuring for the exiles. Moreover, though the recall did send a message about political unity in the face of a common threat and may have gone some way to heal rifts within the *dēmos* among those who were politically at loggerheads, it may also have stirred up former resentments.

Recalling the exiles was not merely about healing old wounds and letting bygones be bygones, however. It also served a very practical purpose. The *dēmos* may have feared that the ostracized would ally themselves with the Persians, as those of the Peisistratid faction had done.[29] No less important, their services would be of considerable value in the upcoming campaign, since political prominence and military expertise were closely linked. We know of two ostracized politicians, Xanthippus, the father of the famous statesman Pericles (aged thirteen at this time), and Aristides, later known as "the Just," who were appointed generals at the elections held in February/March 480 for the year 480/79. Both fought at Salamis.

Lastly, the decree required the Council and the generals "to make an appeasement offering [*arestērion*] to Zeus, Athena, Nike, and Poseidon Asphaleios [Securer]." This probably took the form of a lavish sacrifice. It was required because the Athenians were about to remove sacred objects from their sanctuaries for safekeeping on Salamis, including the olive-wood statues of Athena Polias, and possibly one of Athena Nike, housed on the Acropolis.[30] Such was the need to economize that it seems likely the Athenians drastically curtailed their great civic festivals. The greatest of all, the Panathenaea, was celebrated in July or August on the occasion of Athena's birthday. Its climax was the presentation of a new *peplos* or woolen robe to the old wooden image of Athena Polias. The festival culminated in a huge sacrifice performed on the Acropolis.

The First Evacuation

The first evacuation began either in the winter of 481 or in the early spring of 480, just before Xerxes had begun moving his troops across the Hellespont. It was to be one of the largest exercises of its sort ever attempted by a city-state, involving the relocation of a civilian population that may have been close to 100,000. No text indicates how the Athenians planned to undertake such a complex operation beyond the bare bones preserved in the Decree of Themistocles, so we are left to ourselves to work out the details. The evacuation must have entailed an interruption in all farming activity, including sowing and harvesting, and this would have had severe consequences for those living from day to day. Besides, the state coffers were empty—the building of the fleet had exhausted them—so the evacuees had to finance their transportation and resettlement themselves.

The Assembly probably assigned responsibility for the evacuation to the 139 demes or local territorial districts into which the city and the countryside were divided. Such a complicated undertaking could hardly have been handled at the state level. A deme was a miniature *polis* and had the administrative structure to organize its members and all those living within its territory much more efficiently than the state could. Those citizens of a particular deme who were living elsewhere—a not uncommon practice—probably obeyed the injunctions of their deme of residence. The overall responsibility for the evacuation would have been entrusted to the demarchs, officers appointed by lot with wide-ranging powers, who were expected to represent and enforce decisions taken by the *dēmos* or township they represented. As such they served as "the crucial pivot between the spheres of local government and central government, deme and *polis*," as David Whitehead puts it.[31] The demarchs no doubt relied on the services of junior officials, perhaps specially appointed for the task, and consulted with their deme assemblies. The exercise must have required close cooperation between neighboring demes.

A prearranged order of evacuation was surely put in place to prevent the chaos that would have ensued if everyone had arrived at the coast at the same time. Clearly it would have made sense to evacuate the outlying demes first, though it is also possible that the order was determined by drawing lots. There was probably an interval of days if not weeks between the passing of the decree and the beginning of the evacuation to give the demarchs time to plan the departure. Even so, we may question how orderly the evacuation was. Compelling anxious families to adhere to it in practice would have been a challenge.

Before forsaking their homes, their shrines, and their dead, the evacuees hastily buried all their valuables, hoping to retrieve them when they returned. This would have included pottery with figured decoration, glass bowls, small terracotta images of their gods, and, in a few cases, hoards of coins. Some evacuees probably stripped their houses of wood as well, partly because doors and their like were valuable handcrafted items and partly because, being highly combustible, they made their houses more vulnerable to arson from the enemy.[32] Thucydides tells us that when the Athenians evacuated the Attic countryside on the eve of the Peloponnesian War in 431, they took with them everything that was made of wood, not only furniture but also doors, frames, and shutters. They could do this relatively easily in 431 because their final destination was either Athens or the Piraeus. In 480 it was a much bigger undertaking since they were leaving Attica altogether. Only the wealthy would have been able to take furniture and furnishings with them, either by paying a hefty surcharge to convey it on someone else's vessel or by transporting it on one they owned themselves.

Thucydides reports that in 431 the Athenians "conveyed their flocks and beasts of burden to Euboea and other neighboring islands."[33] What happened to their flocks and beasts of burden, not to mention their pigs, goats, and chickens, in 480? It certainly would have made sense to convey the bulk of their livestock to Salamis, since existing supplies on the island would have been inadequate to feed the refugees for more than a few months. The claim that Herodotus puts into the mouth of Artemisia, queen of Halicarnassus, to the effect that the Athenians sheltering on Salamis had no grain, though something of an overstatement, may have been reasonably accurate.[34]

Most of the evacuees probably heaped their possessions on the backs of slaves or on handcarts pulled by slaves. They then began making their halting progress toward the coast. Slowest moving were the elderly, pregnant women, and small children. Their plight was rather similar to that of the Parisians, who began leaving the capital in June 1940, as soon as they learned that the German armed forces were approaching. Though a few rode on donkeys and fewer still traveled in ox-drawn carts, the majority had to undertake the journey on foot.

Those living on the coast who either owned a boat or had the means to purchase a place on board presumably sailed directly to Aegina, Salamis, or Troezen. Most, however, made their way to Phaleron Bay. Though the work of fortifying Athens's future port, the Piraeus, had begun as early 493, the project had lain in abeyance for many years, so it is questionable whether many of the ships that transported the evacuees out of Attica were able to dock there.

The outlying demes were more than thirty miles from Phaleron, and by the time the refugees arrived, many must have been exhausted, dehydrated, and footsore. Had you stood on the Acropolis among the ranks of those who steadfastly believed that the oracle had bidden you to trust in its defenses, you would have seen numerous groups snaking their way to the coast from points north, south, east, and west, skirting Athens, creating enormous dust clouds in their wake.

What the refugees did for refreshment en route to the coast is anyone's guess. Perhaps there were temporary stations along the way where they could buy food and drink, or perhaps the wealthy shared their produce, or perhaps the state organized convoys of refreshment, just as the Peloponnesians did in advance of the Battle of Plataea the following year. Probably some refugees fell by the wayside, while others turned back in despair. We can hardly suppose that there were any medical facilities available en route.

Having arrived at the coast, the evacuees waited their turn to board, living perhaps in makeshift tents. We don't know how food and water were distributed to them. There is no sizable river in either Phaleron or the Piraeus, where most were awaiting conveyance, so drinking water must have been fetched from wells, an extremely laborious and labor-intensive process. Human waste extended along the shoreline and floated in the sea. Families were split up, since the evacuees were going to be dispatched to different locations. Women and children, heading for Aegina and Troezen, were presumably ordered to gather on one side of the beachhead; the elderly, who were being transported to Salamis, on the other. There was no knowing when—or even if—families would be reunited. Many elderly must have feared they would never see their children and grandchildren again.

For days on end the narrow channel between Attica and Salamis was filled with vessels ferrying evacuees across to the island or further away to Aegina and Troezen. This, however, was not the end of their travails, for once the evacuees had been conveyed to their destination, the same logistical problems awaited them as before. They had to be assigned a place to bed down, as well as to be provided with food and water. Though the *dēmos* must have worked out in advance some plan of relocation, to a large degree the refugees probably had to scramble for themselves.

Even those heading for Troezen were probably evacuated by sea. We're not told what types of vessels were used. Certainly the Greeks were familiar with ships that were capable of transporting warriors to the battlefield—the so-called Catalogue of Ships in book 2 of the *Iliad* demonstrates that. As early as 490 we hear of the Persians having specially constructed ships known as *hippagōgoi* or "horse-transporters," which they used as floating horseboxes.[35] Very possibly the Athenians had built similar types of vessels, which they now used for transporting the evacuees. They also availed themselves of their triremes, which, when manned for battle, were rowed by 170 oarsmen, though that number could have been much reduced to accommodate passengers. As triremes did not have a deck rail, many of the passengers would have had to sit on the benches, taking care not to obstruct the rowers. We should bear in mind, too, that even a slight shift in balance would have risked causing the vessel to tilt precariously and fill with water, so they would have had to remain very still throughout the voyage. This would not have been a problem when they were being ferried across the Straits of Salamis, but it was a serious liability if they were being transported to Aegina or Troezen. In addition to triremes, the Athenians had an unknown number of penteconters, whose capacity was about a quarter the size of a trireme.

Merchant craft of various sizes were also available to the Athenians, and it is probable that these contributed significantly to the transporting, shuttling back and forth across the strait, and perhaps crossing to Troezen and Aegina. If so, we should imagine an evacuation along the lines of that undertaken by the British army from Dunkirk during World War II in June 1940, with trawlers, drifters, tugboats, and even yachts participating. Herodotus claims that the Athenians sent their wives and children to Troezen, but it seems more likely that most refugees were transported to Salamis, due to its proximity.

What happened to the tens of thousands of slaves? Probably many of them vanished into the countryside without trace, once they saw their owners distractedly preparing for departure. Most, however, for a variety of reasons, including loyalty, docility, and fear, accompanied their masters and mistresses to the coast. Very likely many of the able-bodied had already been conscripted into the navy. Thousands would fight at Artemisium and again at Salamis. A minority, namely those deemed essential to the welfare and survival of their owners, probably remained with their owners. Could the average Greek survive without the services of a slave? Many slaves would also have been needed to organize the refugee camp on Salamis. The so-called industrial slaves, both those working in the silver mines at Laurium in southern Attica and those working in the quarries on Mount Pentelicon and Mount Hymettus, were probably conveyed to the coast under armed escort.

The philosopher and biographer Plutarch, ever the moralist, evocatively describes the scene on the shore when the evacuation, which he fancifully suggests was accomplished in a single day, was taking place.[36] He tells us that "as the *polis* set sail"—a powerful phrase to indicate the scale of the evacuation— "the spectacle filled some with pity, others with admiration at the daring of the move, as the Athenians dispatched their dependents in one direction and themselves crossed over to Salamis, oblivious to the shrieks, tears, and embraces of their nearest and dearest. The many elderly, who had to be left behind, aroused compassion, and tame and domesticated animals, too, added to the commotion by displaying heartrending affection for their owners, running along beside them and howling as they embarked."

It is perhaps an insignificant detail amid such terrible human misery that household pets had to be abandoned on the shoreline. And yet it adds greatly to the poignancy of his description. A dog belonging to Xanthippus, the father of the future statesman Pericles, supposedly paddled alongside the trireme that was transporting its master to Salamis, only to expire as soon as it reached dry land. A revered spot on the island, which was known as Cynossema or the Dog's Tomb, allegedly marked the grave for centuries to come.[37] And what happened to Xanthippus's dog might have happened to many, as they swam alongside their owners' vessels till the effort proved too much.

The refugees were not only abandoning all that was most precious and most sacred but also interrupting the traditional cultic behavior that their ancestors had practiced for centuries. True, they could still perform rituals on behalf of their gods to a limited capacity when abroad, but there was no way they could conduct rites on behalf of their dead. The dead could be venerated and tended only in the vicinity of their tombs, since they were dependent on the living for offerings of food and drink. Tomb cult signaled a vibrant and vital connection between the living and the dead, which was now, temporarily, sundered.[38]

Salamis, as I've indicated, probably received the largest number of evacuees. Rocky and mountainous, the island has an area of only thirty-six square miles, compared with approximately one thousand square miles belonging to Attica. First occupied in the Neolithic period, it was colonized by Aegina, then briefly occupied by Megara, and finally, after a prolonged war, became an Athenian possession, probably during the rule of the tyrant Peisistratus, in the second half of the sixth century BCE. For reasons that have never been satisfactorily explained, Salamis was not included in the democratic reforms carried out by Cleisthenes in 511/10, so it never hosted any demes. Probably as today, those who lived on the coast were primarily engaged in fishing, while those who lived inland were farmers. Martha Taylor is of the opinion that the island supported a citizen (i.e., Athenian) population by 510–500 BCE at the latest, though she also points out that there may have been an indigenous population living alongside the immigrants.[39] We cannot gauge even the approximate size of the population before the influx of refugees, but it is safe to say that it now swelled to many times its former size. Since this evacuation probably took place before the end of 481, many of the refugees were destined to become long-term residents of the island, some remaining nearly two full years, even if they briefly returned to the mainland after Xerxes' departure from Greece.

Presumably the Athenians shipped as much grain to the island as they could, both to feed the population for as long as possible and, no less important, to deprive the Persians of supplies of food. But in truth there probably wasn't much grain available, as Artemisia's spies later reported, since there had been little time to gather in the harvest. We don't hear of any reserve stocks kept in readiness by the state. Any animals that the refugees couldn't take with them they would have slaughtered. As soon as they arrived at their destination, the refugees probably began sowing crops.[40] In consequence, the island now became more intensely cultivated than ever before.

We are not told how the evacuees were settled. It would seem logical, however, that the local inhabitants were called upon to host them. The largest settlement in this period was on the eastern side of the island facing the coast of Attica on the so-called Punta Peninsula near the modern town of Ampelakia. It was in Ampelakia Bay that the Battle of Salamis would later take place. Those who could not be accommodated at the settlement were presumably settled in a refugee camp or camps along the eastern shoreline, which took on the appearance of tent city, though some refugees may have preferred to occupy the western side of the island so as not to be exposed to the gaze of the Persians. The distribution of the refugees would have depended largely on the availability of fresh water. Today there are no rivers on the island, and it is unlikely to have been well supplied with fresh water in antiquity, so water probably had to be shipped in amphoras from the mainland to the west side of the island at the point where the land is narrowest. In addition, steps had to be taken to protect all water sources from pollution to prevent the spread of waterborne diseases. The Athenians also had the task of guarding the entire coastline against a possible landing by the Persians. This task may have fallen to the elderly, who were conscripted into a kind of home guard.

All those Athenians who held magisterial office were also evacuated to Salamis, which now became the headquarters of the Athenian state as well as of its military operations. This included all the members of the Council of 500, though it may be that they continued their deliberations in the Agora till the second, emergency evacuation. Everything of value was also conveyed to the island, excluding the treasures that remained under lock and key on the Acropolis.

How did the infrastructure of Salamis cope with the influx of tens of thousands of evacuees?[41] Did the refugees spread out over a large area and form individual settlements? How many sought refuge among Salaminian households? In the modern world refugees are most commonly accommodated in a single refugee camp, not least because of the difficulty of distributing supplies of food over a large area. Martha Taylor has suggested that previously uncultivated land on the island was now cleared to feed the increased population.

It is vital that refugees are settled as quickly as possible. Was water rationed? If it was, this risked putting the population in grave danger, since water is needed both for drinking and for washing. Was food also rationed, or was each Athenian free to purchase or otherwise acquire as much as he needed? If the latter, this might well have led to tension and disagreement between the rich and poor, accompanied no doubt at times by violent scuffles.

How hygienic were the conditions in which the refugees lived? That would have depended on various issues, such as whether the water supply remained largely uncontaminated, how sanitation was handled, the degree of overcrowding, and the quality of their diet. Refugee camps tend to be extremely unhealthy environments. We also need to take into account the high degree of psychosocial stress to which displaced persons are inherently subject, greatly increased in this instance by the fact that the refugees faced the very real possibility of being massacred in the event of defeat at the hands of the Persians. In sum, the evacuation put enormous strain on the economic, social, and environmental structure of the island. What made the situation more taxing for all concerned, evacuees and Salaminians alike, was the fact that there was no knowing how long the evacuees would be living on the island.

There is one bright spot to this otherwise melancholy picture. Plutarch tells us that the women and children who were dispatched to Troezen received a warm welcome.[42] Before they arrived, the Troezenians passed a law that they would "support them at public expense, give two obols to each family each day, permit the boys to pluck ripe fruit everywhere, and hire teachers to educate them." These measures indicate that the Troezenians expected the refugees to be with them for some considerable time—perhaps even, in the worst case scenario, indefinitely. Rarely in history have refugees been accorded such a privileged status. Indeed, the warmth of their reception sounds almost too good to be true, though there is no particular reason to doubt it. Plutarch even supplies the name of the man who introduced the proposal—an otherwise unknown Nicagoras.

Troezen was a tiny *polis* compared with Athens, and its resources must have been severely stretched to accommodate the refugees, making its welcome all the more remarkable. We should not, of course, rule out the possibility that the Athenians offered some kind of sweetener to make their hosts more amenable and accommodating. Even so, the handing over of their wives, their mothers, their sisters, and their children to strangers was a highly unusual act of trust— or perhaps simply a mark of desperation. We do not know how many family groups were billeted in Troezen, though the number may well have exceeded the availability of households to accommodate them. If so, refugee camps must have been set up here, just as on Salamis.

It would be interesting to know whether the evacuees were as cordially received on Aegina. We are not told which section of the population was transferred to this destination. Given the fact that hostilities between Aegina and Athens had only recently been suspended because of the war, however, there was probably some friction between the host population and its guests.

The Fall of Northern Greece

The Greek coalition had taken the decision to block Xerxes' advance by land at Thermopylae, the gateway to central and southern Greece, and by sea at Artemisium. The distance between the two was thirty-five miles as the crow flies, though rather longer by water. It chose this location in part to try to secure the loyalty of the Boeotians, who were threatening to medize. So toward the end of August, an army of five thousand troops, including three hundred elite Spartans and an unknown number of helots, moved north under the command of King Leonidas I, as Xerxes continued his incursion south. It is worth bearing in mind that Leonidas was in his fifties, possibly his late fifties. This is striking, given the fact that in the Greek world people aged much faster than they do today and that life expectancy for a man, approximately forty-five years of age, was correspondingly much lower.

The pass at Thermopylae was so narrow according to Herodotus that there was room for only one cart to get through at a time. This meant that the numerical superiority of the Persians would be neutralized. It also helped the Greeks that their spears were longer and their armor more solidly constructed than the Persian equivalents.[43]

Eventually, however, a Greek traitor called Ephialtes—the name means "Nightmare"—showed Xerxes how to attack the Greeks in the rear by taking a steep and narrow mountain track. Pausanias claims that, had he not done so, "Leonidas and the few he led to Thermopylae would have prevented Xerxes from catching a glimpse of Greece and burning Athens."[44] Though this would hardly have been true in the long run, it is testimony to the belief, still current in Roman times, that had the three hundred not been betrayed, they could have beaten off the challenge from Xerxes' expeditionary force.

Once again, poor reconnaissance undermined the effectiveness of allied resistance. Realizing that it was no longer possible to hold out against the Persians indefinitely, Leonidas dismissed the rest of the Greeks, apart from the Thebans, whose loyalty he questioned; the Thespians, who refused to abandon their post; and the helots, who obviously had no choice in the matter. He took the decision to resist, according to Herodotus, "because it was dishonorable for him to depart, whereas if he remained he would leave behind a great reputation and Sparta's prosperity would not be destroyed."[45]

The Greeks—contrary to the modern tradition, as we have just seen, they were not solely Spartans—were slaughtered almost to a man, but only after inflicting severe damage on the invaders. Herodotus puts the number of Persian dead at twenty thousand, though this is highly questionable (not least since Xerxes allegedly concealed the bodies from view, according to a story preserved by Herodotus).[46] "Go tell the Spartans, thou who passeth by, that here obedient to their laws we lie," runs the epitaph written on behalf of the Spartan dead by Simonides in John Dryden's memorable translation.[47] Herodotus further tells us that Xerxes ordered the head of Leonidas to be cut off and impaled on a stake. This may have been in retaliation for the execution of Darius's envoys. What happened to the rest of the Greek dead is not recorded. Only after the Persians had been driven out of Greece a year or more later were the Spartans able to return and accord them their proper due of burial. However, forty years would pass before Leonidas's supposed remains were repatriated. Henceforth each year the Spartans delivered a speech over his tomb and held a contest in his honor.[48]

Perhaps a day or so later the Greek fleet engaged the Persians at the straits facing Artemisium, off the northern coast of Euboea. Commanded by the Spartan admiral Eurybiades, the fleet comprised 271 triremes and nine penteconters and was manned by over 50,000 naval personnel. About half of the ships belonged to the Athenians. It was greatly to the advantage of the Greeks that perhaps as much as a third of the Persian fleet had been wrecked by a storm shortly beforehand. Even so, the Persians still heavily outnumbered the Greeks, probably by a margin of about three to two.

Though the outcome of the battle was indecisive and though the Greeks were able to inflict heavy losses on the Persians, they now had no option but to withdraw and allow Xerxes free passage toward the Peloponnese. So they headed south on their battered triremes, fearing they would be overtaken by the enemy. As many as half of all the Athenian vessels were disabled.[49] To deceive the Persians into the belief that they were bivouacking on Euboea overnight, the Greeks beached on the island and lit campfires. In this way, metaphorically speaking, they stole a march on the enemy under cover of darkness. Probably, too, the Greeks used the fires to make a halfhearted effort to cremate their dead. Peter Green graphically describes the scene:[50] "Gaps in oar banks and on rowing-benches testified to the ordeal they had so lately undergone. Rams were cracked and sprung from their timbers. Hulls, stove-in dangerously near the water-line, had been roughly plugged with sail cloth. A mess of blood and tangled cordage still littered the decks. The wounded lay wherever they could find an empty space." Such was the likely aftermath to any naval battle in antiquity, even though few triremes are likely to have been sunk beyond recovery. And we should not ignore the fact that the Persian navy faced a similar reality. On its way south and at Themistocles' suggestion, the Greek navy put in at watering holes and chalked messages on the rocks urging the Ionians who were serving with Xerxes to desert. Then it headed for Salamis and berthed in anchorages on the east coast of the island in full view of the refugees along the shore.

In the event, Xerxes took a few days to recover before continuing his journey south. He had to repair his ships, tend the wounded, and dispose of his dead. Despite the belief among some Persians in the cult of Ahura-Mazda, which required that the dead be exposed to the elements so that the flesh could decay, most if not all were probably inhumed. Herodotus tells us that Xerxes played a trick on his own men, however. He ordered that nineteen thousand of the twenty thousand dead should be buried in a trench with leaves heaped on top of them and that the remaining one thousand should be left on the battlefield. He did this so that his sailors, whom he now invited to cross over the strait to view the scene, would conclude that his casualties at the Battle of Thermopylae had been relatively light. Herodotus writes, "Xerxes' trick about the corpses deceived no one for it was ludicrous."[51] Perhaps the historian learned of it many years after the event from an Ionian who had served under Xerxes. We do not know how much effort Xerxes made to recover the dead who perished at sea.

When his army had rested sufficiently, Xerxes continued on his march south. It was now nearing the end of August. The distance from Thermopylae to Athens is about 140 miles. An army moving over rough terrain might be expected to cover ten miles per day at most. Xerxes did not, however, head directly for Athens. Instead he ordered his army to cause as much destruction as it could along the way. It was a tactic designed to breed fear and panic among the Greeks at large. Among his prime targets were the Phocians. The Phocians had refused to join his side because of their hatred of their neighbors, the Thessalians, who had medized. It wasn't principle, in other words, but *phthonos* or "grudge, resentment" that dictated their allegiance. All twelve Phocian townships were destroyed in consequence. Sanctuaries as well as dwellings went up in flames, including a wealthy sanctuary of Apollo at Abae, where the Phocians had dedicated statues seized from the Thessalians following a victory some years earlier.[52]

Most of the Phocians managed to flee before the Persians arrived, some to Mount Parnassus, others westward to Amphissa. Xerxes gave free rein to his soldiers—or more plausibly to his recently acquired Thessalian allies—to do their worst. For the most part Herodotus leaves it to his readers to imagine the scale of the devastation, but he does provide us with one gruesome detail: he tells us that the Persians gang-raped Phocian women and that many of them died as a result, though we may suspect that the chief perpetrators of this monstrous crime were the Thessalians.[53] By now Xerxes' army was less than fifty miles from the northern borders of Attica. Despite heavy losses at Thermopylae, it was still formidable, since more and more Greeks joined the Persian cause the further south the king advanced.

After the destruction of Phocis, Xerxes dispatched a contingent to Delphi with orders to set fire to the Temple of Apollo and carry off its most valuable votive offerings. Herodotus alleges that as the contingent approached the sanctuary, a mighty voice boomed out, sacred arms emerged from the temple of their own accord, and a thunderstorm broke out. This caused two rocks to be detached from the Parnassus range and come crashing down, killing many men. As a result, the Persians lost their nerve and fled in panic.[54] Or at least this is the report that the Delphic authorities circulated after the war to explain why their sanctuary escaped destruction, and such was the esteem in which the oracle was held that Herodotus did not see fit to question it. In the aftermath the report of divine intervention could be used to excuse Delphi's survival, though this does not explain the rock fall, its effects visible in the sanctuary of Athena Pronaia (In front of the temple), approximately half a mile from the main complex of buildings.

The Second Evacuation

John Lazenby goes so far as to say, "For the Greeks the Thermopylae-Artemisium campaign was a disaster."[55] This was particularly so for the Athenians. Very possibly some citizens had refused to obey the first summons to evacuate, clinging to the hope that Xerxes' forces would be repulsed before they got within sight of Attica. The report of Thermopylae and Artemisium, borne first perhaps by beacons and later in more detail by runners, gave them a wake-up call. No force on earth could now deflect Xerxes from his intent to invade and conquer their land. The anxiety of those remaining in Attica became all the more acute, as Xerxes intended, when they learned of the terrible punishment that he had handed out to the Phocians.

So a second, emergency evacuation took place. Or at least that is what seems most likely. Though Herodotus, Diodorus, and Plutarch describe only this emergency evacuation, it is inconceivable that the whole population could have been spirited out of Attica in advance of the arrival of the Persian army in what was probably no more than a week. More likely, the evacuation that had taken place before Thermopylae-Artemisium had been on a much larger scale than this last-minute scramble.

Herodotus informs us that the Athenians—he probably means the Board of Ten Generals known as the *stratēgoi*—issued a "proclamation" to the effect that "every Athenian should do what he could to save his children and other family members"—a clear indication that the state had limited means to assist the remaining evacuees.[56] Since the *dēmos* was now identical to the men who served in the fleet, the latter had the right to constitute themselves into an assembly, capable of issuing proclamations that were binding on the whole community.

The Athenians pleaded one last time with the Spartans and Peloponnesians to take a stand in Boeotia in defense of Attica, pointing out that they had put the interests of other Greeks first by fighting at Artemisium. In fact, they had even sent their reserve fleet of fifty-three ships, intended for the protection of Attica, to Artemisium. Their appeal fell on deaf ears. As ever, the allies cared little about the fate of Attica, having other strategic priorities. The way they saw it, it made little or no sense to commit a large army to defending Attica, not least because there were too many routes that the Persians might take and the Persians were already on their way. So the allied army withdrew, expecting to be joined shortly by the fleet, and in the interim began building a wall across the Isthmus of Corinth at the point where it was just less than five miles in width. Some 30,000 men labored day and night, bringing stones, bricks, wood, and baskets of sand to the site.[57]

The Athenians had been abandoned. Xerxes' advance guard would arrive within forty-eight hours. There wasn't a moment to lose. If it reached the coast before the evacuation had been completed, it would seriously disrupt operations. Indeed, it might even succeed in aborting the mission altogether. According to Plutarch, some of the Athenians who had not yet evacuated said that "if the only course available was to give up their city and stick to their ships they were so despondent that they were no longer interested either in victory or in saving their own lives, if it meant abandoning their temples and the tombs of their fathers."[58] The picture that Plutarch paints is not implausible. It echoes Vergil's description in *Aeneid* book 2 of the elderly Anchises, Aeneas's father, who refused to leave Troy as the Greeks set the city on fire in the belief that he had nothing left to live for. Only a sign from Jupiter restored his flagging spirits and gave him the courage to live another day.

Now, too, we are told, a sign from the gods induced those who were still unwilling to go into exile. Plutarch tells us that Themistocles had been so despondent at being incapable of persuading his compatriots to leave that he appealed to "divine signs and oracles," just as a dramatist might employ the well-known theatrical device known as a *mēchanē* or crane to give the audience the impression that a god was descending to earth from the sky (more familiar to us in the Latin phrase *deus ex machina*).[59] Pious Athenians believed that a giant snake, sacred to Athena, protected the Acropolis. The goddess's identification with a reptile indicates that her origins were partly chthonic—that is to say, that she belonged to the earth as well as to the sky. Herodotus tells us that the sacrificial cake that the Athenians put out for the snake to consume had been left untouched and that according to Themistocles this proved that "the goddess had abandoned Athens and was showing them the way to the sea."

Once again Themistocles' interpretation won over the waverers. Finally convinced that Athena had abandoned the Acropolis, "the Athenians made haste to remove all they had." Or perhaps not quite all of them made haste. In his biography of the politician and general Cimon, son of Miltiades, the hero of Marathon, Plutarch states that even now many Athenians did not wish to confront the Persians by sea. So Cimon ascended the Acropolis in the company of his fellow *hippeis*—citizens, that is, who were sufficiently wealthy to own a horse—and dedicated his horse's bridle to Athena "in the belief that Athens at that time had need of sailors, not cavalry." He and his followers took some shields that were displayed as trophies in her temple in place of the bridle. Plutarch continues: "After praying to the goddess, Cimon went down to the sea and became a source of encouragement for many Athenians."[60] It was a commendably patriotic gesture. A lesser man would have exploited the situation to his political advantage since Cimon was no friend of Themistocles. He might have seized the opportunity to change the course of public policy, but he evidently saw no alternative but to put his faith in the navy.

Some youthful hotheads, who saw the surrender of Attica as an act of cowardice that cast aspersions on their manhood, contrasting as it did so starkly with the heroic last stand of the Spartans at Thermopylae, probably still resisted. There is a tradition reported by the Aristotelian author of the *Constitution of Athens* that the Council of the Areopagus offered to pay each sailor eight drachmas, and that it was this bounty that enabled the fleet to be manned. Since the fleet numbered more than two hundred ships, each of which was manned by two hundred sailors, this amounted to over fifty-three talents—a very considerable sum of money. We don't hear how the Areopagites raised this sum—perhaps we are to suppose they used the treasure from the Temple of Athena on the Acropolis or even paid it out of their own pockets. They allegedly took this initiative after the generals, in utter despair, had proclaimed that everyone should look after his own safety. Thus it was, we are told, that the Council of the Areopagus "was the cause of the naval battle at Salamis" since the state would not have been able to enlist enough sailors without their help.[61] This pro-aristocratic tradition is highly dubious. Herodotus doesn't indicate that the generals were in a state of panic before the battle, and it is unclear why able-bodied seamen had to be bribed to fight when the lives of their families were at stake.

Many of the Athenian ships that had limped back after Artemisium were in urgent need of a refit, so not all could have been used for the evacuation. Themistocles made an urgent appeal to the Greek fleet, drawn up on the beach of Salamis, to assist. Indeed, there would have been no particular reason for it to anchor at Salamis other than to convey the remaining population out of Attica, as Herodotus notes.[62] At this point, Troezen and Aegina were too long a haul, so presumably the only recourse was to ferry the remaining evacuees to Salamis.

When they saw smoke rising from the farms that the Persians had destroyed, those still awaiting to be conveyed to the island must have become more desperate. A few scuffles may have broken out as the last of the refugees scrambled for a place on board the remaining ships. Not everyone complied of course. No evacuation is ever total. We hear of five hundred Athenians whom Xerxes captured on his advance and shipped off to Samos, where they served as slaves. Their identity is unclear, and why they remained behind a mystery. They were perhaps part of a larger number of Athenians who had sought refuge in the hinterland or on the tops of mountains.

-III-

The First Burning

The Persians Arrive

Xerxes entered Attica in mid- to late September, some four months after he had led his army across the Hellespont. His advance force had arrived about five days earlier. His scouts had no doubt told him that the population had evacuated, so he was hardly surprised to find his entry unopposed. Eager to exact vengeance for the burning of Sardis, as well as to demoralize the Athenians, Xerxes instructed his men to inflict maximum damage. Aeschylus tells us that this had been their pattern of behavior as they advanced through hostile territory. The Persians, he writes, "did not respect the images of the gods, burned temples, leveled altars of the gods, uprooted sacred precincts, and reduced everything to rubble."[1] The work of destruction must have slowed down his advance considerably. A prime target was the estates of wealthy aristocrats. The Athenian exiles in his train no doubt directed him to the richest pickings in order to get even with their political enemies.

There is no surviving report of Xerxes' arrival in Athens. Earlier in the journey, as we saw in the previous chapter, Herodotus described him riding in a chariot or being conveyed in a horse-drawn carriage.[2] Now, however, he presumably rode horseback. Quite likely he maintained his army in three columns as he entered Attica so that it could wreak more havoc. As Athens came distantly into view, the victor's prize seemed finally within his grasp. Wasn't the land his, seeing that the enemy had abandoned it? Only the Acropolis was defended, as his scouts had surely informed him days earlier.

Did Xerxes think that the Athenians had simply given up, just as the Phocians had done a few days ago? Though it is certain that he had learned of Athens's naval buildup in the late 480s, it still must have taken him by surprise to meet no resistance.[3] It would have been eerie to set foot in a city whose only occupants (if any) were the very elderly, the very sick, and those at death's door, together with any who refused to abandon them. All that Herodotus says of this deeply charged moment is that the Persians captured the city "when it was deserted." He does not tell us at what point Xerxes ordered it to be burned or whether he bothered to inspect the city before torching it. Certainly it would have offered little to impress the ruler of cities like Persepolis and Susa.

The Persian fleet, which had left Artemisium about six days after the naval engagement, was instructed, like the infantry, to inflict devastation during its voyage south. So after destroying townships on Euboea, it began ravaging the east coast of Attica. One of its targets was the deme of Rhamnous, which lies just to the north of Marathon. Here the Persians destroyed a small archaic temple. They also ravaged Brauron, site of an important sanctuary of Artemis, which lay to the south, and carried off its cult statue to Susa.[4] Though the archaeological evidence is inconclusive, John Camp thinks it is "virtually certain" that the Persians destroyed the predecessor to the present Temple of Artemis as well.[5] At Cape Sunium, the southernmost tip of Attica, they set fire to Poseidon's uncompleted temple, which was located high up on a rocky promontory. Having rounded the cape, the Persians advanced toward Athens and drew their ships up onto the beach in Phaleron Bay, no doubt under the anxious gaze of the evacuees on the island opposite and, indeed, of the Greek fleet that now protected them.

The Persian army was in more or less total control of the Attic countryside, apart perhaps from hidden pockets of resistance in the hills that were made up of men who were ready to fight to the death, should the enemy try to dislodge them.

The Siege of the Acropolis

The city, too, was bereft of defenders. There may have been a few Athenians lurking in the shadows ready to knife or strangle any Persian who happened to drop his guard, but we hear nothing of them. The decision to resist the Persians by sea meant that the circuit wall could not be manned.[6] Had the Athenians made an attempt to defend it, all who were guarding it would have been massacred. Siege warfare was a brutal and messy business in antiquity, so once the city fell, the besiegers typically unleashed their pent-up fury on the besieged.

Some pious Athenians, however, confident in their interpretation of "wooden wall," had, as we've seen, stayed behind to defend the Acropolis. From Neolithic times onward, the hill had functioned not only as a sanctuary but also as a fortress. In fact, it may well have been a fortress long before it became a sanctuary. In the early fourteenth century BCE, what may have been a Mycenaean palace complex was built on the summit together with a massive wall, remains of which can be seen to this day. By the eighth century at the latest, there are indications of worship both on the summit and in the niches along its sides.

The Acropolis features prominently in several episodes of Athenian history. An Athenian aristocrat named Cylon occupied it circa 632 in the hope of establishing a tyranny. After he had agreed to terms of surrender, many of his supporters were impiously murdered.[7] The tyrant Pisistratus, after establishing himself in power with the aid of mercenaries, strengthened the fortifications and made the Acropolis his residence by means of a garrison circa 547. His son and successor Hippias was blockaded by the Spartans and forced to evacuate in 510.[8] Hippias eventually escaped to the court of Darius I and, as we saw, was present with the Persian forces at Marathon. Finally, when the Spartan king Cleomenes was seeking to establish an oligarchy in Athens in opposition to the reformer Cleisthenes in 508, he took refuge on the Acropolis and sustained a siege that lasted three days before being forced to withdraw.[9]

There was, therefore, a long history of resistance associated with the rock, albeit largely unsuccessful for the besieged. We are told the defenders now barricaded themselves against the invaders "by means of doors and timbers." This suggests that the defenses were in poor condition, though they certainly had plenty of time to improve them. We don't know how many Athenians volunteered to remain on the Acropolis or were compelled to do so by virtue of their office. Herodotus tells us that they were only "a few" in total and that these included "the treasurers of the temple and some impoverished people, who . . . believed that they had discovered the true meaning of the oracle that the Pythia had delivered, namely that . . . this place and not the ships was impregnable."[10]

Were the defenders perhaps hoping for a miracle, along the lines of the thunderstorm and the falling rocks that had reputedly saved Delphi by scaring the invaders away? We know why the treasurers of the temple were there. They had no choice. The Council and Assembly had ordered them to guard the god's possessions. This raises the question why the treasure was not removed to Salamis for safekeeping. And what about the impoverished? Why did they remain? What was their investment in defending the Acropolis?

Though strength of religious belief would have been an important factor, it is possible that some Athenians didn't have enough money to cover the cost of their sea passage out of Attica. The author of the Aristotelian *Constitution of Athens* tells us that the members of the Areopagus paid each rower eight drachmas, but this as we've seen is likely to be a later fabrication, intended to enhance the reputation of that aristocratic body.[11] An even more improbable story has Themistocles searching through the belongings of the evacuees purportedly for a missing ornament belonging to the cult statue of Athena and then appropriating for public use all the money he found.[12]

Herodotus tells us that when the Greeks learned that the Acropolis had been taken, they were so demoralized that their commanders gave the order to flee. This suggests that the Athenians were still committed to defending the Acropolis even though they had determined to face the Persians at sea. He also says that Xerxes was frustrated "for a considerable time" by the spirited resistance of the besieged.[13] None of this makes sense if the only people defending the Acropolis were the treasurers and the impoverished. There is a distinct possibility, therefore, that the Athenians left behind a garrison, which they hoped would have a good chance of withstanding the assault. It was by now the third week in September, and the campaigning season was drawing to a close. If the garrison could hold out for a few weeks, the Persians might be forced to retire, since their fleet would be at risk moored on the open roadstead of Phaleron.

From their vantage point on the Acropolis, the defenders would have had an excellent view of Xerxes' outriders galloping through the plain, leaving a trail of dust behind them. Later they observed the army advance toward the city, burning villages and farms. They also had a view of the Persian fleet headed toward Phaleron, with destruction following in its wake.

It may have been on arrival in Athens that the Persians defiled wells belonging to private houses, just as later they despoiled the spring of Gargaphia, which, as Herodotus reports, was the only available water supply for the entire Greek army before the Battle of Plataea.[14] As Kathleen Lynch has speculated, "Perhaps the easiest way of defiling wells was to use them as latrines or heap horse feces into them" since "either would render the water impotable for the returning

The Areopagus

homeowners."[15] She further observes that this tactic would strengthen the Athenian belief that the enemy had polluted their city.

Xerxes now ordered his men to take up position on the Areopagus, a small hill that lies a short distance to the west of the Acropolis. The name perhaps commemorates the fact that it was here that the war god Ares stood trial for the killing of Poseidon's son Halirrhothius. Alternatively, it may derive from *ara*, "curse," hence the "Hill of Cursing." As the hill could accommodate only a minute fraction of his army, Xerxes probably ordered only a small handpicked contingent to gather there.

Apparently Xerxes took personal charge of the siege. This was, after all, a highpoint in his campaign. Under his direction his men wrapped coarse fiber around their arrows, set the fiber alight, and then fired their arrows at the wooden barricade. Herodotus perhaps learned of this detail either from the Peisistratid exiles who were accompanying Xerxes or from other Greeks who were serving in his army, since there were no Greek survivors from the siege. In his words, "The fortification having betrayed them, the defenders faced the utmost of extremity."[16] Even at this juncture, however, and though the Peisistratid exiles tried to negotiate terms, the defenders refused to surrender. Instead they hurled down boulders and column drums and whatever else came to hand upon the attackers. It's uncertain exactly how long they were able to hold out—previous sieges of the Acropolis had lasted as many as five days— but it was sufficient for Xerxes "to be at a loss what to do for a considerable time," as Herodotus reports.[17] Meanwhile the Greek fleet, anchored off Salamis, was fearing the worst.

Eventually some of the attackers found a way up "right in front of the Acropolis, but behind the gates and the path that leads up, where no one was guarding and where no one would have believed anyone could scale the rock, just below the sanctuary of Aglaurus, who was the daughter of Cecrops."[18] Herodotus's testimony is confusing because the place "right in front of the Acropolis" suggests the west slope, whereas the reference to the sanctuary of Aglaurus indicates the north.[19] Realizing that resistance was futile, several defenders hurled themselves off the rock. Nicholas Hammond says they did this "rather than live to see their city enslaved," but they may also have feared that the Persians would exact terrible revenge to make an example of them.[20]

Believing that all was now lost, some of the defenders took refuge inside one of the buildings—we're not told which one. Those of the enemy who had scaled the rock opened the doors of the Old Propylon or Gateway and admitted their companions. What greeted their gaze was the venerable Temple of Athena Polias (Of the City), as well as column drums rising from the pre-Parthenon building site, and numerous statues dedicated to gods and goddesses. Perhaps the priestess of Athena, decked in her splendid robe, stood at the entrance to her temple, a venerable figure striking momentary awe in the invaders. Or had she taken her cue from Athena's sacred snake and joined the evacuees at the last moment? After all, if the snake in its divine wisdom had adopted the motto *sauve qui peut* (save yourself if you can!), why shouldn't her human representative follow suit?

Herodotus at this point calls the Athenians "suppliants," which means that they formally placed themselves under the protection of Athena and identified themselves as her property. The Greek word *asulia*, which is what we somewhat misleadingly translate as "asylum," is better translated as "inviolability," the literal meaning being "the condition of not being plundered or abducted [from a sanctuary]." Much good it did them. The Persians slaughtered everyone indiscriminately.[21] It was an act of gross sacrilege, guaranteed to incur divine punishment, and it later provided a useful explanation for why Xerxes' expedition failed. Herodotus does not tell us what happened to any women who had sought shelter on the Acropolis.

The burning of the Acropolis now began. The oldest building to go up in flames was the Archaios Neos, the "Old Temple" of Athena Polias, mentioned a moment ago. This had been built in the Doric order of architecture during the reign of the tyrant Hippias circa 520 BCE. It probably stood on the site of the ancient palace of Erechtheus, one of Athens's legendary early kings. Its pedimental sculptures, made of poros, a type of coarse limestone, depicted lions attacking bulls and creatures from mythology, including a triple-bodied monster.

The Temple of Athena Polias housed the ancient olive-wood statue of Athena, which had probably been removed to the safety of Salamis. We know the statue escaped destruction because it still existed in the second century CE. Since it was "considered by all to be the holiest object since before the time of the unification of Athens," as the travel guide Pausanias puts it, its loss would have been devastating.[22] A wooden statue of Hermes, "allegedly a dedication by Cecrops," a mythical king of Athens, may also have been removed, along with a cult statue of Athena Nike (Victory).[23] The altar of Athena, which lay to the east of the temple, was destroyed.

Another temple in the Doric order that burned down was the Older Parthenon—the Temple of Athena Parthenos (Maiden), perhaps also known as the Hekatompedon (Hundred-footer).[24] This had been begun either before or more likely soon after the victory at Marathon and was still under construction at the time of the invasion. Dark pinkish marks still visible in the stone are thought to indicate where the scaffolding went up in flames. The Older Parthenon lay to the south of the Temple of Athena Polias, roughly on the site of the present Parthenon, which later used its foundations and many of its parts. It is thought to have had a peristyle or surrounding colonnade consisting of six columns on the ends and sixteen on the sides. A temple to Athena Nike, located at the southwest corner of the Acropolis, which had been built around the same time, was also razed. Its foundations lie buried under its classical replacement.[25]

Yet another victim was the Old Propylon—or at least as much of this entrance gateway as had been built. Work on the gateway had probably begun soon after the Battle of Marathon. Though fairly modest in size compared with its vast, ornamental successor dating to the 430s, it was the first structure on the Acropolis to be made of Pentelic marble.[26]

There is also mention in an inscription of archaic *oikēmata* (buildings) constructed in the Doric style, in which moneys belonging to the gods were stored. They probably resembled the so-called *thesauroi* or "storehouses for treasure" that can be seen at international sanctuaries like Delphi and Olympia. No traces of them have been found but they probably lay to the west of the present Parthenon. These, too, were destroyed.

The reason why buildings made of stone could burn is that they contained a great quantity of combustible material. Their roofs were made of wood, and once they caught fire, the burning planks would crash to the floor. In addition, since many buildings were still under construction, there was considerable scaffolding in place, and all this would have added to the force of the conflagration. The heat buildup inside each building became so intense that the walls would crack, thereby quickly reducing the whole edifice to a pile of rubble.[27]

Xerxes' soldiers also vented their fury on the hundreds of marble sculptures that stood out in the open, which they knocked over and smashed.[28] These sculptures are sometimes referred to as the "Perserschutt," a German word meaning "Persian rubble." The ones that had been erected recently were still brightly painted, whereas those that dated back in some cases to the second quarter of the sixth century were dull and weatherworn. Most had been dedicated to Athena. Particularly impressive was a large group of draped marble maidens known as *korai*. The sculptural type of the *korē* or maiden took the form of a standing female worshiper, who was depicted tightly clutching her skirt with one hand and extending the other, as if in the act of making an offering. The Persians also hacked about a commemorative monument that had been erected to Callimachus, architect of the Athenian victory at Marathon. As Jeffery Hurwit writes, "The history of Archaic Athenian art was essentially compressed into this one place, and it was this accumulated achievement that in just a few hours' time fell victim to the Persian massacre of images."[29] For some reason, the Persians overlooked a seated statue of Athena by a sculptor of the archaic period called Endoios, which Pausanias reports seeing on the Acropolis, evidently still intact in the second century CE.

As for all the statues that were made out of gold, silver, or bronze, these were melted down or, in a few cases, transported to Persia. One that Xerxes salvaged was a spectacular bronze chariot group, which the Athenians had dedicated on the Acropolis as "a tithe from their victory over the Boeotians and Chalcidians" in 506. His men also smashed a great quantity of black- and red-figure pottery dedicated to Athena and tossed their remains into the fire. They probably stuffed into sacks all the bowls, plates, and cups made of gold, silver, and bronze. This was the "treasure" that the treasurers of Athena had sacrificed their lives to protect.

Excavation of debris from the Persian destruction on the Acropolis.
Courtesy of the Metropolitan Museum of Art, Gilman Collection,
gift of The Howard Gilman Foundation, 2005.

The Persian sack resulted in much more than the mere destruction of in-
comparable works of art. As Tom Holland memorably put it, "The great store-
house of Athenian memories, accumulated over centuries—the city's very
past—was wiped out in a couple of hours."[30] "A couple of hours" may be a slight
exaggeration, but it was probably an afternoon's work at most. It's easy to de-
nounce Xerxes' act as vandalism, but it is important to realize that he saw it as
payback for a previous act of desecration. The king had exacted revenge on the
Athenians for the burning down of the Temple of the Mother Goddess in Sardis eighteen years earlier. Perhaps, too, he saw himself as acting as the representative of Ahura-Mazda in crushing the worship of false gods. He was also

signaling the fact that the Athenians were bereft of their gods. In such dire straits, would they still have the heart to fight on?

It is impossible to know what effect the destruction of the temples on the Acropolis had on Athenian belief, but it must have been devastating. Even so, given the size of the Persian invasion force, only the most fervent would have expected the gods to save their city by means of a miracle. Faith, no matter how unshakable, does not require the pious to believe that their gods are capable of moving mountains. After all, Athena's snake had seen the shape of things to come and, in making its hurried departure from the Acropolis, was itself acknowledging the limits of divine intervention. And even if Themistocles had bribed the priesthood to falsify the claim that the reptile had gone off its feed, this didn't alter the fact that pious people would be expected to take their cue from the snake.

Moreover, although the sack of the Acropolis would have been deeply demoralizing, we should not assume that most Athenians believed their gods had abandoned them. On the contrary, they might have concluded that they and their gods were suffering an equal affront. The burning of the Acropolis might even have emboldened them to exact vengeance on the perpetrators on their gods' behalf. Plato later referred to Athena as "our dear maiden and mistress who is among us," and it may be that the Athenians felt as protective of their goddess as she was believed to be protective of them.[31] The heart of Greek religion eludes us, but that does not justify us in regarding it as a spiritual vacuum.

Casting his eyes back on the smoldering ruin as his army advanced toward the coast, Xerxes might have reflected that a major part of his mission had now been accomplished.

The Destruction of the Agora

Herodotus mentions only the destruction of the Acropolis—he says nothing about what happened to the rest of Athens—but the Agora, the civic, political, and commercial heart of Athens, situated to the west of the Acropolis, suffered grievously too. Probably it was torched before nightfall on the same day that the Acropolis went up in flames. The destruction was so complete that not a single archaic building escaped serious damage.

Among those edifices reduced to rubble was a large irregular structure with numerous small rooms known as Building F, which lay at the southern end of the west side of the Agora. The structure may have served as a palace for the Peisistratid tyrants. Also severely damaged was the Royal Stoa, situated at the northwest corner of the Agora, which served as headquarters of the king archon, the annually selected magistrate in charge of religious affairs. The Old Bouleutērion or Council House, which accommodated the five hundred members of the Boulē, also suffered serious damage. Further evidence of the sack has been found in seventeen wells in the Agora: debris that includes pieces of sculpture, architectural fragments, and broken pottery. It's also likely that the Persians destroyed the predecessor to the present Temple of Hephaestus on Colonus Agoraios, the low hill to the west of the Agora, since traces of burning have been found on the site.[32]

The most celebrated work of art that Xerxes removed from the Agora and took back to Susa as war booty was the sculptural group representing the Tyrannicides, Harmodius and Aristogeiton.[33] The Athenians honored the two men on the grounds—entirely false according to Thucydides—that they had rid them of the hated Peisistratids by murdering Hipparchus, the brother of Hippias.[34] Both had been killed by the tyrant's supporters immediately afterward. So the statues of the Tyrannicides would have had deep meaning for the Athenians as the embodiment of their democratic principles. No doubt Xerxes fully understood their significance, having been given a lesson in Athenian history by the Peisistratid exiles. Centuries later either Alexander the Great or perhaps the Seleucid monarch Antiochus I, one of Alexander's immediate successors, returned the statues to Athens.

Another sculptural piece that Xerxes took was a bronze statue of a water carrier that had been dedicated by Themistocles when he was water commissioner. The artwork had been paid for from the fines he had imposed on those who had been convicted of diverting and stealing water. Many years later, when Themistocles sought refuge in Persia as an exile, he came across the statue in Sardis and asked the satrap to return it to Athens.[35]

The extent of the destruction meted out to the rest of the city is unclear. We don't, for instance, know what was the fate of the Olympieion, the Temple of Olympian Zeus, which stands on the southeast side of the city. The temple, one of the most grandiose building projects ever undertaken in the Greek world, had been begun by the Peisistratids in the late sixth century. Since work on it had long since been abandoned after the demise of the Peisistratids, the Persians may have decided that it wasn't worth destroying, added to which they might have been discouraged from damaging it by the supporters of tyranny, who saw it as showcasing their ambition to return to Athens.

The city devastated, or as much of it as Xerxes thought appropriate to his long-term goals, the Persian infantry began marching toward the Peloponnese "that very night" as Herodotus tells us—that is to say, on the very night that the Acropolis had fallen.[36] It is worth bearing in mind that Xerxes might have concluded that there was much to be gained by preserving the livelihood of his future subjects, rather than reduce their city to rubble. Greece north of the Peloponnese had already been incorporated into his empire.

Herodotus tells us that the king dispatched a messenger to the court at Susa reporting his success. When his subjects heard the news, they joyfully threw myrtle branches on the roads, burned incense, and performed sacrifices.[37]

Xerxes' Second Thoughts

However, the day after the sack, as Herodotus would have us believe, Xerxes had a dramatic change of heart. His conscience, or simply fear, got the better of him. So he ordered the Athenian exiles in his entourage to go back up onto the Acropolis and perform sacrifices "in the customary manner." Herodotus speculates that the change of heart came to him either as the result of a dream or because he felt remorse. It is not difficult to see why from a Greek perspective Xerxes would have been feeling remorse. He had committed two of the worst impieties, the destruction of a sanctuary and the massacre of asylum seekers. He had not only incurred the anger of the gods but also unleashed pollution. He had therefore put himself in the same league as the cursed Alcmaeonid *genos* or noble kin group, whose ancestor Megacles had in the seventh century slaughtered those seeking refuge at the altar of Athena.[38]

A more likely explanation for the sacrifice is that Xerxes realized that he had outraged the religious sentiments of the Athenian exiles upon whose goodwill he was counting. Indeed, his destruction of the Acropolis might be seen as a personal insult to the Peisistratid faction, since it was Hippias who was credited with elevating the sanctuary to the ancient equivalent of a World Heritage Site.

The emotions of those exiles who returned the next day to the grim and blackened ruin is not recorded. We may picture them picking their way with difficulty among the charred and blackened corpses, the smashed columns, and the toppled statues, smoke still rising from the ashes. Especially heart-rending must have been the sight of the remains of those slain at the altar, some perhaps bearing traces of their priestly apparel. Only after the bodies had been removed could a sacrifice be performed.

At a site of special veneration, however, they reportedly discovered a miracle. The olive tree that Athena had caused to grow inside the sanctuary of Erechtheus when competing with Poseidon for the guardianship of Attica, though destroyed in the conflagration, had already put forth a fresh shoot one and a half feet tall. The precise measurement was no doubt calculated to lend credence to their claim.[39] Very likely the report of the miraculous sprouting was kept under wraps once it had been reported to Xerxes. Had it reached the Athenians on Salamis, it would have given hope in the ensuing struggle by presaging the city's eventual revival.[40] Both the tale and the tree became taller over time. Pausanias tells us that he heard the tree had grown three feet overnight.[41] Whatever we make of the story, the exiles were clearly signaling to Xerxes that, though allied to the Persian cause, they remained patriots, loyal to the state and to its foremost deity.

The *Dēmos* Afloat

On the far side of the Straits of Salamis, the tens of thousands of Athenians who had been conveyed to the island, as well as all the rowers in the allied fleet whose ships were beached on the shore, observed with horror as a heavy pall of black smoke begin to darken the sky over Athens.[42] Their anxiety was made more acute by the arrival of the Persian fleet around the same time, which beached in Phaleron Bay. If the refugees were in the least doubt as to the fate of the Acropolis, scouts lighting a beacon from the summit of Mount Aigaleos, situated a short distance to the west of Athens, probably notified them of its fall. We can imagine the dejection and misery. Some would have deduced that the devastation was just desserts for their involvement in the burning of the Temple of Cybele. Herodotus certainly believed that the burning of Athens was brought about by divine retribution, though he does not specifically state that the destruction of the temple in Sardis was the precise cause.[43] The predicament of the evacuees was now dire in the extreme, their fate wholly dependent on the fortunes of the allied fleet.

In the meantime, the Peloponnesian infantry, numbering about thirty thousand, having learned of the defeat at Thermopylae, was assembling at the Isthmus of Corinth, there to await the Persian assault. Under the supervision of Cleombrotus, the youngest brother of the Spartan king Leonidas I who had fallen at Thermopylae, the Peloponnesians hastily began building a wall, or perhaps more accurately a reinforced earthwork, between the ports of Cenchreae and Lechaeum, where the isthmus was narrowest. They had delayed taking this defensive action until after the Thermopylae-Artemisium campaign, even though the intention to defend the Peloponnese had always been their primary objective. They perhaps calculated that, had they begun building the wall earlier, they would likely have reduced the size of the coalition, since those members whose territory lay outside the Peloponnese, Athens in particular, would have realized that no serious attempt to resist Xerxes north of the isthmus was in the plan. Very likely the wall or earthwork wasn't finished until the following summer. A stretch of seventeen hundred meters extending along a ridge has been plausibly ascribed to it.[44]

Events now happened fast. The allied fleet and army had become two separate entities no longer under joint command. To aggravate matters, the fleet, which according to Aeschylus, our earliest source, numbered around three hundred ships, threatened to fissure.[45] The allies, we are told, were downcast by the burning of the Acropolis, and this makes sense only if we assume that there was a reasonable expectation that the defenders could withstand the Persian siege. So when the allied fleet saw the Acropolis in flames, some of its commanders, instead of waiting to discuss what course of action to adopt next, simply hoisted their sails and sailed off. Herodotus uses the word *thorubos* to describe the scene at this point. It suggests a state of utter confusion with voices raised in anger and alarm.[46]

The commander of the contingents that remained at Salamis, some twenty in all, held an immediate council. They agreed to sail south and block the Persian fleet at the Isthmus of Corinth, thereby abandoning the Athenians to their fate. Though united (sort of) in a common cause, they had little concern for the welfare of a single member of their coalition. And if any of them needed to justify their action, they could argue that the Athenians had already given up on Attica. Attica was a lost cause. This decision reached, the Greek commanders retired to their ships for the night.

We hear only of the reaction of the Greeks to the destruction of Athens. We know nothing about what the evacuees were feeling at this moment. It's likely that they weren't informed about the decision of the council, presumably in order to avoid causing them to panic. That is because an elderly Athenian named Mnesiphilus paid a visit to Themistocles after he returned to his ship that night and asked him what had been discussed at the council. We don't know whether Mnesiphilus had been chosen by the evacuees to represent their interests, but he had close ties with Themistocles. Apart from the fact that they were both demesmen of Phrearrioi, Plutarch claims that Themistocles was "a zealous admirer" of Mnesiphilus—the word he uses is *zēlōtēs*, which gives us our word "zelot"—though he disparagingly describes him as a sophist.[47]

Herodotus claims that when Themistocles told Mnesiphilus that the allies were determined to fight a naval battle at the isthmus, the latter pressured him to go at once to Eurybiades, the Spartan commander of the allied fleet, and have the decision reversed. Mnesiphilus pointed out that if the fleet withdrew to the Peloponnese, the coalition would dissolve, and the whole of Greece would be destroyed. This, incidentally, is the same argument that Herodotus puts into the mouth of Artemisia, queen of Halicarnassus, when Xerxes is deliberating about whether to fight a naval battle at Salamis. Do not fight in the straits, she urges him, since there is nothing to be gained. But if you bide your time, within a short period of time the coalition will simply dissolve.[48]

Themistocles, we are told, "was delighted by Mnesiphilus's suggestion and without replying went straight to Eurybiades' ship." Are we seriously to believe that such an obvious tactic hadn't occurred to him already? More likely, as Donald Lateiner has suggested to me, this is a product of the anti-Themistoclean propaganda that began to circulate soon after the Persian defeat and that resulted in Themistocles' ostracism at the end of the 470s.

Themistocles now urged his commander in chief to call another council. This story, too, gives rise to suspicion, since the course of action that he was advocating was in clear violation of the unanimous decision that had been taken by his fellow commanders only hours ago. However, Eurybiades allegedly acceded to his request and summoned the commanders again. If what Herodotus relates is true, they must have obeyed the summons with extreme reluctance and misgiving. A more likely suggestion, to cite Donald Lateiner again, is that this anecdote is intended to emphasize the fact that none of the allies were initially supportive of the decision to fight at Salamis. Naturally Herodotus's sources would have wanted to deny any credit to the Spartan commander, given the hostility that arose between Athens and Sparta as soon as the war ended. Themistocles merely "repeated verbatim to Eurybiades what he heard from Mnesiphilus as if it were his own invention," Herodotus tell us, though he grudgingly concedes that the politician "embellished the idea a great deal."[49]

Persuading Eurybiades was one thing; persuading the coalition quite another. While Themistocles was passionately arguing his cause to his fellow commanders, the Corinthian Adeimantus interrupted him and insolently declared that he refused to listen to any proposal put forward "on the recommendation of a man who has no fatherland and is *apolis*" (i.e., "one who is not a member of a *polis*" or "one who has no *polis* to be a member of").[50] What Adeimantus meant was that Athens, following the evacuation of its population, no longer enjoyed the status of an independent polity since its citizens had no homeland. He could scarcely have delivered a more humiliating insult. He was intimating that an Athenian general was no longer entitled to a voice or place in the Greek war council.

Themistocles angrily retorted that his *polis* and its land were greater than that of the Corinthians and that if the allies withdrew and made no attempt to defend the Straits of Salamis, then the *polis* would set sail for Siris, a city in the instep of southern Italy, "which has long been ours and which an oracle prophesied we would settle."[51] Themistocles's use of the word *polis* in this context is instructive. All able-bodied Athenians were currently serving at sea, including most of the hoplites, who were doubling as rowers. The *dēmos*, in other words, *was* the fleet. It was no exaggeration, therefore, to describe the fleet as a *polis*.

This discussion, as reported by Herodotus, is almost certainly a fabrication. No one took minutes of war cabinet conferences in the ancient world, and it is unclear where he got his information. He doesn't claim to have interviewed anyone who was present. Most of those who attended were very senior officers and they were probably dead by the time Herodotus began doing research. So his source must have been secondhand at best. Since the report is highly favorable to Themistocles, the most likely candidate is one of his descendants, hardly the trustworthiest source. As John Lazenby points out, the historian gives us "what an intelligent and more or less contemporary Greek thought might have been said."[52] This, however, does not alter the fact that Herodotus may be representing accurately a division of opinion within the war council. Even so, the extremely negative light in which Adeimantus is portrayed doubtless reflects postwar anti-Corinthian propaganda.

There is a more specific issue to address. Did Themistocles seriously contemplate the permanent resettlement of the entire citizen body at this late stage? Admittedly Herodotus had previously noted that during the debate about the "wooden wall" the *chrēsmologoi* recommended "abandoning Attica and settling somewhere else."[53] But that was months ago. The impracticability of implementing an operation of this magnitude on the eve of a battle is mind-boggling, particularly since the refugees had already been dispersed to three separate locations. If Themistocles had tried to carry out such a resettlement, only a fraction of them could have been transported. Tens of thousands would have been abandoned and have perished in consequence. But why Siris of all places? The answer may have something to do with the fact that the *polis* was perhaps unoccupied at this time—a not uncommon occurrence—even though we know that it was inhabited forty years later.[54] It is also possible that Themistocles had a personal connection with Siris, since he had named one of his daughters "Italia."

But though Themistocles' threat seems like a desperate stratagem and a pretty implausible one at that, had the Greek fleet deserted Athens at this point, no other course of action would have been available. It is easily overlooked that the Greek *polis* was inherently portable, since our literary sources emphasize the natural predilection of its citizens for permanence and continuity. Permanence and stability were not invariably the norm, however. Many communities either underwent relocation or at least seriously considered that option.[55] As the Athenian general Nicias aptly put it in 413 when seeking to encourage his army shortly before its surrender to the Syracusans, "Men make the *polis*, not walls or ships devoid of men."[56]

There were, moreover, recent precedents for an overnight evacuation. That was exactly what other Greeks whose villages and towns lay in Xerxes' path had done. The Phocians had withdrawn to the heights of Mount Parnassus, from which they would have been able to watch the flames rising from their homes as the invaders did their work of destruction, while the Plataeans had simply melted into the countryside. Though these particular communities probably expected to return to their homes once the Persians had passed through their territory, others relocated for good.

A dramatic example of relocation involves the inhabitants of Phocaea, modern Foça—not to be confused with Phocia—an Ionian city on the western coast of Anatolia that lies to the north of the Gulf of Smyrna. By a circuitous route its population migrated to southern Italy just before the Persians were poised to take the city around 545. There was a difference, however. It's likely that the Phocaeans had penteconters rather than triremes at their disposal, and these warships were designed to be rowed by fifty men, but with a capacity of perhaps eighty. Being more stable than triremes, they would have been able to carry passengers over a much greater distance. There's another consideration to bear in mind. Phocaea's population was tiny compared with that of Athens. Certainly Themistocles made the threat in part to rattle the allies and bring them into line, since Athens's 180 ships made up more than half the total Greek fleet.

It doesn't take much to imagine the fate of the noncombatants in the event of a naval defeat. The fleet would not have had time to land on Salamis and embark any civilians. Instead, it would have had to leave the evacuees to their fate. Sailing across to Salamis the morning after the battle, the Persians would quickly overwhelm any opposition and round up all those on the island. Either the evacuees would have been massacred, as happened to the Samians in the late sixth century and to the Milesians during the Ionian Revolt, or they would have been deported.[57]

The best that the battered remains of the Athenian fleet could have hoped to achieve after a defeat was to head straight for Aegina. Pursued by the Persian navy, however, it would hardly have been in a position to mount a full-scale evacuation from that island. Within days the island would have been taken. The women and children in Troezen had at least some chance of survival since the town lies to the south of the defensive wall that the Greeks were building across the Isthmus of Corinth. But once the Persians broke through the wall, which was likely since there would have been no sizable fleet to oppose them, the women and children would have been shipped off to Persia as slaves. To conclude, it's not inconceivable that Themistocles did indeed have a plan of resettlement in mind as a very last resort, though we may still wonder whether he ever voiced such a suggestion in the Assembly.

In any event, the commanders in the council couldn't be sure that Themistocles would not follow through on his threat, so they took him at his word and backed down. Even so, Themistocles sensed that they might still get cold feet and decide to withdraw. "Cold feet" was perhaps putting it mildly. Herodotus speaks of the Peloponnesians being gripped by "fear and terror." And, as he points out,[58] with good reason: "The Peloponnesians were terrified because there they were immobilized on Salamis, on the point of fighting at sea on behalf of a land that belonged to the Athenians, facing the prospect after defeat of being trapped and besieged on the island, and thereby leaving their own land unprotected." They had a point. What sense did it make to remain at Salamis, given the fact that their capacity to defend the Peloponnese would be seriously compromised if they were defeated?

The next morning Themistocles ordered a slave called Sicinnus, whom he had entrusted with the welfare of his children, to inform the Persians that the Greeks were divided, that they intended to slip away secretly that night to the Peloponnese, and that if they, the Persians, blocked their exit route on both sides of the straits they would win a magnificent victory. We are told that "the commanders of the barbarians" who received Sicinnus found his message "credible."[59]

This anecdote, too, is seriously problematic. Sicinnus did not, according to Herodotus, seek an audience with the king himself. Rather the decision was initiated by the Persian commanders as a group. Is that likely, given the top-down nature of Persian autocracy? There is a more serious issue. Would it not be remarkable if either Xerxes or his high command accepted at face value this extraordinary reversal of allegiance on Themistocles' part without questioning it in any way? Why on earth would they trust Themistocles—the leader of a community whose "enmity must have been intensified by the recent devastation of their land and the destruction of their temples," as Hignett points out?[60] And what plausible reason could Themistocles give for his change of allegiance? Herodotus says that he told Sicinnus to declare that his master "happened to be well disposed toward the Great King and wanted his side to prevail over that of the Greeks."[61] Would that have been enough to persuade the Persians to change their plan of action at the last moment? In defense of the veracity of the anecdote, there is a distinct possibility that Themistocles already had ties with Persia, and if so, this might have made Sicinnus's mission more likely to succeed. This is suggested by the fact that when he went into exile he eventually found refuge at the court of Xerxes' successor, Artaxerxes I.

Improbable though the anecdote may seem, no other explanation has come down to us as to why the Persians chose their particular strategy.[62] Herodotus reports that after the war Themistocles had Sicinnus made a citizen of Thespiae and bestowed much wealth on him—a detail that lends further credence to the account.[63]

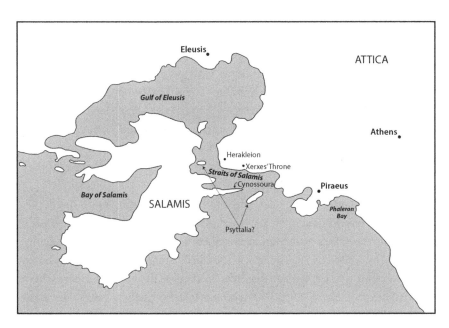

Salamis and the Straits

Whatever induced the Persians to attempt to entrap the Greek fleet in the straits, once it became dark Xerxes ordered his sailors to embark and move into position to guard the eastern exit. Throughout the night the ships' captains no doubt made the fleet sail back and forth across the channel. The sailors were under strict orders to perform this maneuver in absolute silence so that the Greeks would be taken completely by surprise when they sailed out. Aeschylus reports that the king threatened to execute all those responsible if any Greek ship managed to escape.[64]

As the hours dragged by, mental as well as physical exhaustion began to set in. It can hardly be doubted that this significantly contributed to the Persian defeat the next day. For eight hours or more the commanders strained to hear any sound of movement from the shore opposite. Long before dawn they must have realized that there was to be no mass breakout and that they had been right royally deceived. There was nothing they could do, however, but remain hunched over their oars. Only Xerxes could countermand the order, and Xerxes was on dry land. No one would dare to disobey the king, least of all under threat of decapitation. The Greeks meanwhile spent the night ashore on Salamis, lodged in bivouacs or perhaps makeshift tents, and had plenty of time to eat and relieve themselves. When dawn began to break, they had an immense psychological and physical advantage.

The details of the battle are very difficult to work out. As Peter Green puts it, "Despite its momentous importance, Salamis must be regarded as one of the worst-documented battles in the whole of history of naval warfare."[65] Aeschylus's account is sensationalist. Herodotus, who was never at his best in attempting to describe a battle, is of little help. He claims that the battle was "bound to turn out the way it did" simply because the Greeks were disciplined and the barbarians disorderly.[66] A very brief account is to be found in Diodorus Siculus, who probably derived it from the fourth-century historian Ephorus.[67] What sources Ephorus used is unknown, but there is no reason to believe that they predated Aeschylus or Herodotus.

The Greeks weren't very disciplined in the hours leading up to the battle, however, as Herodotus admits. When Aristides, one of the exiles who had been recalled by the terms of the amnesty, sailed from Aegina and with difficulty breached the cordon of ships to inform the allied commanders in the early hours of the morning that the Persian fleet was blockading their exits, he found them engaged in a "combat of words."[68] Herodotus fails to explain how Aristides managed to slip through the cordon, but that doesn't alter the fact that the members of the Greek council were still arguing on the morning of the battle. The word that Herodotus uses here for their "combat of words" is *ōthismos*, which means literally "a thrusting or pushing." It was often used of shields being thrust against one another during a hoplite battle, the two opposing sides pushing with all their weight and might. In other words, he makes it sound as if the council meeting was on the point of turning into a barroom brawl with the commanders hurling chairs at one another. Even when Aristides tells them that they can't escape because they're completely surrounded, most of them don't believe him, and another argument breaks out. It might have been comical, if so much hadn't been at stake.

Even at the eleventh hour, some of the commanders were still entertaining the possibility of flight. It was only when a Greek ship deserted from the Persian fleet and confirmed Aristides' report that they accepted the inevitable and prepared to do battle, seemingly now without exhibiting any panic. This is pretty remarkable, given their level of anxiety only hours beforehand. Perhaps it helped that just before sunrise, an earthquake occurred. The Athenians took this as a good omen and immediately dispatched a ship to Aegina to convey statues of the descendants of Aeacus to Salamis, in the belief that these heroes would fight alongside them. The statues were presumably placed inside the sanctuary of Ajax situated in the main town of Salamis, since Ajax, who was a Salaminian, was descended from Aeacus. The heroes, or images of them, had to be present to be effective.

As the sun rose from behind the ring of mountains that enclosed Athens and illuminated the straits, Themistocles urged his men to reflect that "both in human nature and in circumstances there is a better course and a worse course, and to choose the former." This seems a curiously abstract observation with which to send combatants into harm's way, though Herodotus claims that of all the speeches delivered before the battle by the allied commanders his was the most effective.[69] He then ordered his sailors to board, as did all the other commanders. Many of them had just said goodbye to their elderly relatives, who now thronged the shoreline, anxious, expectant, and fearful. Rarely in the history of human conflict have there been so many spectators at a battle.

It was almost certainly due to Themistocles that the fleets engaged at the hour that was most favorable to the Greek fleet—shortly before 9:00 A.M., when a southern breeze arises in the straits that causes the channel to become choppy. This made the enemy ships keel and knock against one another since they were crowded closely together.[70] At the same moment the Greeks rowed out from the shore and advanced toward the Persians, singing a paean or battle hymn, as Aeschylus tells us. It would have been an eerie sound, especially if there was still some morning mist obscuring the sight of the Greek ships. Very soon they got the upper hand. Chaos ensued among the Persian ships, and the Greeks pressed home their advantage, charging the enemy amidships and holing them with their bronze rams. Aeschylus tells us the battle raged till sunset—around 7:30 PM, that is, at this time of year—strong evidence of the intensity of the fighting.[71]

Neither Aeschylus nor Herodotus provide figures, but Diodorus, who bases his estimate on Ephorus, claims that more than two hundred Persian ships were lost, compared with only about forty on the Greek side.[72] The scale of the Persian loss is almost certainly exaggerated.[73] The victory had been largely due to the Aeginetans and Athenians. And that's about all one can say with any certainty. The allies had won a stunning victory. They had defeated an armada with a fleet perhaps only half the size. The enemy was forced to withdraw to Phaleron Bay. Xerxes had placed some troops on a tiny island between Salamis and the mainland called Psyttalia, their mission to kill any Greeks who might try to scramble ashore as their ships sank.[74] In the event, the Persians were themselves hunted down and killed.[75]

Decisive though the outcome of Salamis was, the war was far from over. The victory solved nothing in the short term, even if it did tilt the scales in favor of the Greeks. The Persian fleet was still appreciably larger than that of the Greeks, the refugees on Salamis remained at grave risk, the allied commanders were in disorder and lacked a concerted plan of action, and the Persian infantry was poised to launch an attack on the Peloponnese.

It would take another land battle to drive the Persians from the mainland, and that meant surviving the winter with the enemy breathing down their necks.

Xerxes Withdraws from Attica

The outcome of a battle may not be evident until after some time has elapsed. Herodotus tells us that the Greeks hauled up on shore all the wreckage they could, being "prepared for another naval encounter, since they expected the Great King to use again those of his ships that had survived."[76] This indicates that they certainly didn't take it for granted that they had won a resounding victory.

Xerxes watched the annihilation from the comfort of his throne, which had been set up on a headland opposite the town of Salamis, in the foothills of Mount Aigaleos, no doubt close to his army base at Herakleion. Having a bird's-eye view of the battle, he can have been in no doubt of the outcome before the two sides parted for the night. According to Aeschylus, he "wailed out loud when he observed the depth of the horror." Did he? That is perhaps wishful thinking on Aeschylus's part.[77] The dramatist further alleges that when he realized that the battle was lost, he tore his robes—not an easy task one might think—and returned to his camp.[78]

Diodorus Siculus claims that, Xerxes "in his distress blamed the Phoenicians for everything and ordered that they be executed so that those who had proven themselves to be worthless should not slander their betters."[79] This was the same punishment that he had supposedly handed out to his engineers when the cables linking the pontoon bridges over the Hellespont had snapped.

Herodotus states that the king now dispatched a second courier to Susa bearing news of the defeat. "There is nothing swifter that is mortal than a Persian courier," he observes. The system was such that a man and a horse were posted at intervals along the route one day's journey apart, and "neither snow nor rain nor heat nor gloom of night stays these couriers from the swift completion of their appointed rounds."[80] The result was that the second courier arrived soon after the one who had been dispatched previously with news of the burning of Athens. Aeschylus has the courier describe how the Athenians kept striking at the Persian sailors as they floundered helplessly in the water, "just as if they were tunny fish or some other fish you catch in nets."[81] A courier would certainly spare his audience such a grisly detail, though the report itself may be based on an eyewitness report. According to Herodotus, those who had rejoiced in the sack of Athens only a few days earlier now tore their robes and gave themselves over to lamentation.[82] Herodotus is probably borrowing the detail of the tearing of clothes from Aeschylus. Admissions of defeat were not characteristic of Achaemenid monarchs, and there is no knowing how the news—or what news—was relayed back to Susa.

The scene that impressed itself upon Xerxes on the morning after the battle must indeed have been horrific. The channel between Salamis and the mainland, a mile across in places, was thick with corpses, flotsam, spars, and waterlogged hulls. In his play the *Agamemnon*, Aeschylus vividly describes the sea as "blossoming" with corpses after a storm. The metaphor would equally apply to the sight that greeted Xerxes' eyes—the same sight, of course, that the evacuees on Salamis gazed upon. They, too, must have been grief-stricken, doing the rounds of the ships once the fleet limped home at night, seeking their dear ones, either reuniting with them tearfully or learning sorrowfully of their loss. Many had been wounded on both sides, and by dawn the next day the number of dead had no doubt increased.

As Barry Strauss points out, "In the days after the Battle of Salamis, the shores of Attica became the most ethnically diverse graveyard in human history to that date."[83] We do not know whether the Greeks were able to recover many of the dead whose bodies were floating in the channel. They no doubt did the best they could. Presumably they cremated all the corpses of their comrades that were washed up onto the shore, leaving the Persian dead to rot in the water. It is possible that a tumulus at the end of the peninsula known as Cynossoura or Dog's Tail contains the remains of those who fought in the battle.

The Persians by contrast were in no position to sail out into the strait, so most of their dead probably ended up at the bottom of the Saronic Gulf, unrecognizable after four days at most. Herodotus claims that the Persians and their subjects did not know how to swim and so drowned, whereas those who composed the Greek coalition did and so swam to the safety of Salamis.[84] There is, however, no evidence to indicate that Greeks sailors were trained to swim, but, if they were, we might expect Ionian Greeks fighting on the Persian side to be able to swim just as well.[85] Even so, it's not improbable that more Bactrians, Carians, Cilicians, Cypriots, and Egyptians drowned than were actually killed by the enemy.

This was by no means the end, however. The Athenians scarcely had time to breathe a sigh of relief before learning that Xerxes was planning to seize Salamis by building a causeway at the point where the channel between Attica and Salamis is narrowest.[86] Or at least that is what Herodotus claims. Modern scholars have tended to be skeptical of the claim, on the grounds that the seizure of the island with winter coming on would have served no useful purpose at this point in the campaign.[87] It is possible, however, that Xerxes began building a causeway to demoralize and distract the Athenians, while secretly readying his army for withdrawal, which is what Herodotus suggests. We can well imagine that the dismay of the refugees would have been profound at the sight of Xerxes' engineers on the shoreline opposite. Had not they proved what they were capable of at the Hellespont? To make matters worse, the allied fleet had departed soon after the battle. This meant that the Athenian fleet had to remain on full alert, ready to take on the Persians alone should they attempt to invade Salamis.

The face-off lasted a few days at most. And then one morning the Athenians woke up to discover the enemy fleet had slipped away noiselessly in the night. Xerxes may have interpreted an eclipse of the sun that occurred on October 2 as an evil omen sent by Ahura-Mazda. In truth, he needed no such prompting, as the campaigning season was coming to an end, especially for naval combat.

His fleet played no effective part in the war again. It sailed straight for the Hellespont, ordered to safeguard the bridges for Xerxes' return. A few miles out from Phaleron, however, it mistook a promontory for an enemy squadron—a clear indication that it was in panic mode.

The Athenians immediately set off in pursuit, eager to force a second encounter. When they arrived at Cape Sunium, however, they discovered that their quarry had got clean away. So they headed for Andros, an island about a hundred miles east of Salamis by the roundabout sea route, where the rest of the allied fleet had gathered.

As the Athenians sailed off, however, they would have been only too aware that Xerxes' army continued to pose a threat to the evacuees. How long, they must have wondered, would it take his engineers to bridge the channel from the mainland to the island? Probably a few weeks at most. Their separation anxiety must have been acute. And what if the Persian fleet should decide to return? Presumably the Athenians left a small flotilla of swift ships at Salamis, ready to speed to Andros and recall the fleet should the need arise.

Arriving on Andros and entering into discussions with the allied leaders, Themistocles found himself in the same situation as before Salamis. Once again he was desperately searching for an argument that would induce the allies to adopt a strategy to avert a bloodbath for the refugees. He proposed to Eurybiades that the fleet should now chase the Persian fleet north, finish the job it had begun at Salamis, and in this way dispel any fear that Xerxes might launch another attack. This time, however, his proposal fell on deaf ears. Herodotus tells a highly implausible story that Themistocles sent a second messenger to Xerxes, claiming that the Greeks intended to sail to the Hellespont and burn the bridges. Terrified at the prospect of being trapped on the far side of his empire, Herodotus continues, Xerxes broke camp and headed home, instructing his cousin Mardonius to pursue the war in Greece without him. "Even if all the men and all the women in the world had urged him to stay," Herodotus claims, "he would not have done so, so fearful was he."[88] It is a pathetic picture of craven incompetence, intended to contrast strikingly with that of the surly bully boy who had invaded Greece.

The picture of Xerxes being paralyzed with terror is undoubtedly propaganda. A more plausible reason as to why he decided to return home was because of rumors of unrest in some of his satrapies. The decision to leave Mardonius behind was perhaps more political than strategic. He could hardly have expected him to conquer Greece now that the fleet had departed. If, however, his army had retired without any further attempt to do battle with the Greek allied army, Xerxes' prestige as a great king and warrior would have been seriously compromised, as Hignett pointed out.[89]

The allies gave up on pursuing the Persian fleet and, in so doing, infuriated the Athenians, who had been eager for revenge. Instead, they offered to "liberate" Andros, which had previously been subject to the Persians, on condition that its inhabitants pay tribute. The islanders flatly refused to comply, and after a halfhearted siege the allies sailed off. Threatening to destroy them if they failed to pay up, however, Themistocles compelled the inhabitants of Carystus, a city at the southern tip of Euboea a few miles to the north of Andros, and Paros, an island in the Cyclades, to pay tribute. He allegedly did so unknown to the other generals. So much for Greek solidarity.

Herodotus tartly observes that the architect of the victory at Salamis was a man "whose greed could not be satisfied." The charge of venality, even if it had some basis in fact, probably reflected the hostility that Themistocles subsequently incurred.[90] Yet the incident also points—not implausibly—to an unpalatable degree of opportunism, which may well have tarnished the brilliance of his intellect.

-IV-
The Second Burning

The First Homecoming

It was early October, the end of the campaigning season, and the allied fleet now returned to Salamis to divide up the spoils. It was customary for the Greeks to dedicate a tenth portion of the spoils of battle to their gods, and on this occasion they dedicated three captured Phoenician ships: one at the Isthmus of Corinth to Poseidon, one at Sunium to Poseidon, and one at Salamis to the hero Ajax. Herodotus notes that the one in Corinth "was still there in my day."[1] Why didn't the Athenians preserve the two that were in Attica? As trophies of their victory, they later set up a freestanding marble column in the main town of Salamis, probably on the tip of the promontory; another marble structure further south but no longer visible that was noted by travelers in the eighteenth century; and a third on the island of Psyttalia.[2] These would have replaced temporary trophies erected immediately after the battle. Our word "trophy" derives from the Greek word *tropē*, meaning the place where a battle took a decisive turn, and such monuments were dedicated to Zeus Tropaios, "The Turner." In addition, the Athenians made offerings at Delphi and Olympia.[3]

The allies then headed to the Isthmus of Corinth, where their generals held a vote at the altar of Poseidon to determine which of them was "the best."

Herodotus tells us that each general voted for himself first and for Themistocles second, so Themistocles was declared the winner.[4]

Once Xerxes had ruled out an attack on Salamis, his fleet sailed home, and
within a day or so he marched north, escorted by Mardonius. When they arrived at Thessaly, Xerxes prepared to lead the bulk of the army north toward
the Hellespont, while Mardonius selected the pick of the troops to remain there
with him. Mardonius's force is estimated to have numbered sixty to eighty thousand. He now began planning an attack on the Peloponnese in the spring.

By late October, Xerxes had departed from Thessaly, presumably taking the
same route by which he had entered Greece. According to Herodotus, he reached
the Hellespont in forty-five days, though it's not entirely clear whether he is
referring to the journey from Phaleron or that from Thessaly. If Herodotus
means forty-five days from Phaleron, then Xerxes accomplished the journey in
half the time it had taken him to march from the Hellespont, which would suggest that he was in a rush to get back to Asia.[5] This would make perfect sense,
given the onset of winter.

Both Aeschylus and Herodotus paint a gruesome picture of a terrified army
reduced by disease, hunger, and thirst, Herodotus probably borrowing from Aeschylus. Allegedly the army was forced to eat grass and the bark and leaves of
trees, and many died of dysentery and plague.[6] The image is almost certainly
false—"doubtless bearing only the most tenuous connection to reality," as
Briant puts it[7]—being intended to underscore the humiliation of the king's re-
treat, even though Herodotus tells us—a surprising detail—that Xerxes took the
trouble to see that those who fell sick were cared for by the local population.
It's worth pointing out as well that northern Greece, namely Thessaly, Paeonia,
and Macedon, remained loyal to Persia and that he met little or no resistance
along the way, even though he was unable to recover the sacred chariot
of Ahura-Mazda, which he had left behind in Macedon on his march into Greece.[8]
It was only after the army had left the mainland that a rebellion broke out.

By the time Xerxes reached the Hellespont, the bridges over that stretch of
water had been destroyed by a storm, so instead the fleet ferried the army across
to Abydos. The operation presumably took several weeks, not least because
many of the soldiers were exhausted and enfeebled. This, too, was an evacuation of sorts. The king continued on to Sardis, where he spent the winter. Then
in the spring he proceeded to Susa. "Few out of many" would return home, the
Ghost of Darius in Aeschylus's *Persians* had prophesied after the defeat at Salamis, but that is no doubt an exaggeration for dramatic effect.[9] Since he had left
his royal tent behind in Greece with Mardonius, it is conceivable that Xerxes

was intending to return to Greece the next year. Or should we suppose that he was primarily concerned about Mardonius's comfort?

Following Xerxes' departure from Attica, the refugees on Salamis, or at least a sizable proportion of them, returned to their homes—or to what was left of their homes after they had been burned and ransacked. Farmers, the majority of the population, would have been eager to get back to their lands, even though they must have realized that there was a very good chance that Mardonius would return the following spring—as indeed he did. Whatever facilities had been set up for the refugees in the way of tents and shacks on Salamis were presumably left in place. The desire to inspect the devastation and pick among the ruins would have been overwhelming, however, no matter how painful the experience. We can be less sure whether the refugees on Aegina and in Troezen returned. Transporting them home would have been a much more complicated and lengthy process and prudence surely dictated that they should stay put until such time as the entire Persian army had been driven from the mainland, particularly in the case of the women and children in Troezen. So the winter passed with fathers and husbands separated from their wives and children.

No surviving source tells us anything about the naval operation that was put in place to transport the refugees back to the mainland from Salamis. It can hardly have been less complex than the evacuation, and it may well have taken rather longer, given the fact that there was no special sense of urgency. The allied fleet probably returned to Salamis in mid-October. This would have been the moment when most of the refugees on the island were finally able to return to their homes. Whether the Athenians were able to persuade their allies to assist them in the operation is unknown. Possibly they had to do the work unaided, now that they no longer had any leverage over them.

The homecoming must have been extremely traumatic, particularly for those who had been forced to leave behind relatives who were either too sick or too frail to be evacuated. Some may have encountered decomposing bodies in their homes or evidence of Persian savagery in wounds that had been inflicted on those too helpless to offer any resistance. In the countryside those who had been bedridden, if they escaped the wrath of the Persians, may have starved to death. The first duty of the returnees was to give the dead solemn burial. Many graves, too, had presumably been robbed of their valuables, particularly those belonging to the aristocracy, easily detectable as they were by the sumptuousness of their funerary monuments. They contained costly gifts for the dead, including jewelry and precious metals.

It was not only the destruction of their temples, tombs, and homes that the returnees had to deal with, however. Greeks had a strong belief in *miasma*, "pollution," an invisible and deadly force very like a virus that, if unchecked, could attack the whole community, blighting crops and cattle, rendering women sterile, and causing pestilence.[10] To counter it, they routinely performed ceremonies of purification, especially in sanctuaries and places of assembly. The Persians had polluted the city by their presence alone, quite aside from the *miasma* they had caused by the horrific acts they had carried out on the Acropolis.

The Persians had destroyed what they could, but mercifully their occupation had been brief—probably under a month. Food, however, would have been in very short supply. It is doubtful whether the Athenians had had the time or the energy to plant crops and sow seeds before evacuating Attica the previous year. Herodotus tells us that it was Themistocles who urged them to "rebuild their homes and diligently attend to the sowing, now that the barbarians have been completely driven away."[11] Completely? It's highly unlikely that Themistocles was so naïve as to believe that they had seen the back of the Persians. More likely he saw the task of rebuilding and sowing as a useful distraction from their woes.

Themistocles now disappears from Herodotus's narrative. The last sight we have of him is in Sparta in the winter of 480/79, when he is being feted for keeping Athens loyal to the allied cause. We're told that he received unprecedented honors for a foreigner—an olive wreath "for his wisdom and shrewdness," the best chariot in Sparta, and a royal escort to the Tegean border when he departed. It seems he went to Sparta on his own initiative, angered perhaps by the fact that his compatriots were not showing him that degree of appreciation he believed was his due. It may be that his advocacy of a naval strategy no longer found favor with the Athenians. The fact that the Persians were still in northern Greece could well have undermined confidence in his strategy.[12] It is possible too that recommending the rebuilding of Athens while the Persians were still in the offing caused him to become something of a pariah later, when they returned to burn Athens again. Clearly the warm reception he received at Sparta provided fodder for his enemies, of whom there were many. So far as we know, he was never put in charge of the fleet again.

Themistocles nonetheless succeeded in outwitting the Spartans after the war had ended, when they attempted to prevent Athens from rebuilding its city walls (see next chapter). He was perhaps among the first to realize that Persia was no longer Athens's main enemy.

Mardonius's Offer of Alliance

With Xerxes' exit, Mardonius now had free rein in Greece. Yet his initial operation, wintering in Thessaly, proved to be a grave strategic error, since it gave the Athenians a much-needed chance to draw breath and recover their fighting strength. Why on earth didn't he go for the kill? It's difficult to see how the refugees on Salamis could have survived the winter under siege conditions. They might have had to surrender or even to adopt the course of action Themistocles threatened to do before the Battle of Salamis—namely, relocate to southern Italy.

One reason why Mardonius chose to withdraw is that it would have been very difficult to survive the winter in Attica, given the size of his army. But why didn't he leave a few thousand behind to keep the Athenians penned up on Salamis? Had he done so, starvation might have stared them in the face. Perhaps he feared they would be no match for the victorious Athenians. Even so, as Pierre Briant aptly notes, "Persian strategy never ceases to amaze."[13]

Another motive for withdrawal is that he was seeking a diplomatic rather than military solution. It's not inconceivable that Mardonius had chosen to winter in Thessaly in part because he was eager to draw the Athenians into his fold. He was calculating—correctly in Herodotus's viewpoint—that if he had their fleet on his side he could still win the war at sea. Herodotus reports that Mardonius had by now learned that the Athenians were "a numerous and warlike people."[14] If that is true, I can only say that he was a remarkably slow learner. No doubt the historian included this observation to gratify his Athenian readers.

Mardonius was probably counting on the fact that the Athenians were divided about what action to take. He was also aware that relations between them and the Spartans, always tense at best, were under severe strain. The Spartans had made it abundantly clear that they were concerned with the fate of Athens only to the extent of Athens's usefulness. The sufferings of its people registered little with them, if at all. Many Spartans, not to mention Corinthians and other Peloponnesians, might even have thought that it would be no bad thing if Athens were wiped off the face of the earth.

So in the spring of 479 Mardonius sent Alexander I, king of Macedon, to Athens in the hope of winning the city over to his side. We may wonder whether he fully considered the impact of his initiative upon his Greek allies, who would hardly have welcomed the Athenians among their ranks. Mardonius chose Alexander as his ambassador because he was a *proxenos* of the Athenians; that is to say, he was officially empowered to represent the interests of Athenians visiting or residing in Macedon. He could therefore be expected to have considerable influence at Athens, since he had many powerful and prominent friends in the city. Another reason why Alexander might have expected a warm reception was that he had probably sold timber for shipbuilding to the Athenians. In short, he was the ideal ambassador for the Persians.[15]

Herodotus speculates that Mardonius was persuaded to make his approach to the Athenians on advice that he received from oracles, though he provides no details to support this claim. If this is true, it suggests that Xerxes left Mardonius with carte blanche to determine how to bring the campaign to a satisfactory conclusion. It further indicates that Mardonius was initially at a loss as to how to proceed.

We are not told where the Athenians received Alexander, but it may have been in the Agora among the ruins of the Old Bouleutērion, perhaps partially restored so that it could function as before. It was here that the fifty members of the Council or Boulē, who were always on hand to deal with day-to-day business, normally received foreign dignitaries.[16] If so, the Athenians would have been sending a strong signal of defiance to the Persians that, despite the devastation, it was business as usual.

Alexander began by delivering the message that Mardonius had received from Xerxes:[17] "I will forget all the wrongs the Athenians have done to me, so this is what I want you to do, Mardonius. First you are to give them back their land and next let them have other land that they choose in addition, living in freedom. If they agree to my proposal, you are to rebuild all the holy places that I burned down." Alexander then passed on what Mardonius had relayed to him about the wisdom of accepting Xerxes' offer:

> Why be so mad as to wage war against the Great King? You could not possibly prevail or hold out indefinitely. Didn't you see the size of his expedition and what he has accomplished? You've heard how large the army I have with me is. Even if you defeat it—which is inconceivable if you think about it rationally—another many times larger will be coming. Do not therefore try to match yourself to the king, because if you do you will be deprived of your country and on the run forever.

Finally, Alexander, "speaking with goodwill" as he put it, added this commentary in his own voice: "I urge you to accept Mardonius's offer. I know you can't make war against Xerxes indefinitely. . . . The Great King's power is superhuman and his reach extends far and wide. If you do not come to an agreement

while the enemy is offering you such magnanimous terms, I fear on your account because you of all the allies will be devastated since your land lies primarily in disputed territory where fighting takes place."

News (at times) traveled fast in the ancient world, and while Alexander was
still in Athens, a Spartan embassy arrived in the city. Or perhaps the Athenians
sent word to the Spartans in order to alarm them by the prospect that they might
defect to the Persian side. They had every reason to use the Persian offer as a
bargaining chip, in the hope that the Spartans would take on Mardonius before
the Persians invaded their territory a second time. So before they responded
to Alexander they gave audience to the Spartan ambassadors—perhaps even
in Alexander's presence.

The Spartans urged the Athenians not to desert the Greek cause, first on the
grounds that it was they, the Athenians, who were responsible for the war in
the first place—hardly a very compelling argument, even though it was basically
correct—and second because they had always been regarded as the liberators of
other peoples—a more flattering argument but hardly more substantial than
the first. They went on to say that since the Athenians had lost two harvests,
they and their allies would "support and maintain Athenian women and all
other noncombatants for as long as the war lasted."[18] The offer of economic
support would, of course, have been much appreciated, but what the Athenians desperately needed if they were to have any hope of resisting a second
invasion was military aid. Of this there was no mention. In the full awareness
that they were inviting a second invasion, the Athenians instructed Alexander
to bear the following message to Mardonius:[19] "As long as the sun follows its
present course we shall never enter into an agreement with Xerxes. We will trust
in the gods and the heroes, for whom Xerxes showed contempt when he burned
down their homes and statues, and advance against him and defend ourselves."
A rousing riposte indeed. They then turned to address the Spartans as follows:[20]

Sparta's fear that we would come to an agreement with the barbarians was a natural one. Even so we think it disgraceful that you were afraid, given the fact that
you are fully aware of our character, namely that no quantity of gold is sufficient,
no land so beautiful that we would be willing to accept it in exchange for medizing and enslaving the Greeks. There are many compelling reasons that would
prevent us from so acting, even if we were willing. First there are the images and
dwellings of the gods that have been burned down and destroyed, which compel
us to exact the utmost vengeance on the man who perpetrated this act rather than
make a treaty with him. Second there is our shared Greekness. We share the same

blood, speak the same language, hold in common the same shrines and sacrifices, and practice the same customs, and it would not be good for the Athenians to betray all that. . . . However, we appreciate your forethought, the fact that you recognize that our homes have been destroyed and are willing to maintain and support our families. Your kindness is full to bursting, but we will struggle to hold out without inconveniencing you. But seeing the state we are in, send an army as quickly as possible. For it is our guess that the barbarians will invade our land within a short space of time, indeed as soon as they learn that we are not going to do what they asked. So it's time for you to advance into Boeotia to help us before they arrive in Attica.

Scholars have been understandably skeptical about the accuracy of these speeches, believing that the tone of high idealism is *post eventum*. As Hignett notes, however, how could Athens's leaders not have appealed to the patriotic instincts of the people when calling for yet another act of supreme self-sacrifice?[21] The Persian offer might well have been tempting. Some Athenians may have been ready to throw in the towel. Cautious Athenians, however, would have pointed out that the offer was too good to be true. What grounds could they have for trusting the Persians to follow through on their extravagant promises? For them to shift allegiance at this moment would have greatly angered those states that had stood beside the Persians from the start, not least the Thebans, who heartily detested the Athenians.

Herodotus—or his informants—would have us believe that the offer hadn't any appeal. The Athenians were united in defiance. Appeasement wasn't an option. This may well be true. Even so, it is worth noting that he does not tell us how they came to their decision, whether there were any dissenting voices, or who actually delivered the speech.

The Second Evacuation

When Mardonius, on his march south from Thessaly, arrived in Boeotia, the Thebans advised him to use their region as his base and adopt the tactic of bribery to subjugate Greece. He rejected their advice, being possessed by "a keen desire to capture Athens a second time both because of his lack of judgment and because he wanted to notify the king in Sardis by means of beacons located in the islands that he held Athens in his grasp."[22]

Herodotus seems to be suggesting that Mardonius was incapable of sound military judgment, owing both to his anger toward the Athenians and to his jealousy of his superior. That may or may not be correct. The fact remains that the second invasion of Attica, which he now undertook, achieved very little. On the contrary, it merely stiffened Athenian resistance.

Mardonius crossed the border into Attica probably in late June—just ten months after the first occupation by Xerxes. He may have been expecting, even hoping, to face resistance. On his arrival, however, "there were no Athenians to be found and he learned that the majority of them were either on Salamis or with the fleet, so he captured a city that was deserted," as Herodotus puts it.[23] "Capturing a city that was deserted" hardly amounts to a military victory, and there is more than a hint of scorn in that expression. It is not impossible that a close to total evacuation had taken place this time. After all, the reality of what would happen to those who remained had now sunk in.

Herodotus tells us that the Athenians had waited as long as they could before withdrawing in the hope that the Peloponnesians would defend them. When they realized that the Spartans were in no hurry to come to their rescue, they performed a last-minute evacuation.[24] By now they had got evacuation down to a fine art. Once again we know nothing of the details, though on this occasion Salamis was almost certainly the only destination.

The Athenians were furious with the Spartans for having, as they saw it, betrayed them and for allowing the barbarians to invade Attica a second time. They sent an embassy stating this fact in no uncertain terms and urging the Spartans to send their army without delay so that they could face the barbarians in Attica together. It was to no avail. The Spartans delayed receiving the ambassadors for ten days on the grounds that they were celebrating a festival, while at the same busying themselves with the completion of the wall across the isthmus. Meanwhile, the Persian high command took up residence in the ruined city in houses that were still left standing. The rank and file presumably bivouacked.[25]

Mardonius made one last attempt to persuade the Athenians not to yield to what he called their "lack of judgment" (*agnōmosunē*) now that Attica was in his grasp. Interestingly, this is the same word that Herodotus had used earlier to describe Mardonius's own attitude in wanting to take Athens. He sent over to Salamis a Greek from the Hellespontine region named Mourychides in a last-ditch attempt to persuade the Athenians to accept Xerxes' terms. It was the Council of 500, whose members had evacuated to Salamis, which received him. This time the councilors were in a highly belligerent mood. With the exception of only one member, they rejected the offer outright, no doubt pouring scorn on Mourychides for his attachment to the Persian cause.

The single exception was a hapless man named Lycides, who proposed that the offer be submitted to the *dēmos* for its consideration. This seemingly innocuous suggestion might have simply been ignored, had the councilors been thinking rationally. But they weren't. They began to surround Lycides menacingly, egged on by some Athenians who were outside the chamber listening in on their deliberations. Soon the Council had turned into a lynch mob, and Lycides was stoned to death.

Worse was to follow. Lycides' treasonable recommendation that they should put the king's offer to the vote spread throughout the community. It fired up the women, who formed themselves into a posse and went in search of his house. When they got there, they stoned his wife and children to death.

The episode is shocking in the extreme, all the more so because the crime was initiated by Lycides' fellow councilors in an official and sanctified setting. These were no hooligans but officers of the state. Had the *dēmos* sunk to such a low level that it no longer tolerated freedom of speech? Or should we assume that freedom of speech meant something very different to them from what it means to us? What makes the incident all the more disturbing to us is that it was cited repeatedly in the fourth century as an edifying tale of Athenian patriotism.[26] All that can be said in mitigation of the crime is that it speaks eloquently to the intense suffering that the Athenians had been put through, as well as to their inflexible resolve to tough it out at all costs.

It also indicates how strikingly their mood had hardened in the course of ten months. Whereas at the time of the first evacuation there had been those who did not want victory if it meant abandoning their temples and tombs, now everyone—or almost everyone—was united in a common cause. The enemy had done its worst, and to give up at this point would have meant that the previous sacrifices had been for nothing.

Mourychides was allowed to depart unscathed and bear the report of this incident to Mardonius. It's unlikely that the Council members accorded him a formal reply. An account of their action would have been a sufficient answer. Learning of the Athenian "response," Mardonius must have been exasperated. All his good-faith efforts to strike a deal with the Athenians had come to naught. Even now, however, he did not immediately wreak vengeance on the city. In fact, it was only after he learned that the Peloponnesians were marching against him that he decided to withdraw to Boeotia.

It was at this point that he "set Athens on fire and razed it to the ground, demolishing all the walls and the houses and the sanctuaries that were still standing [viz., after Xerxes' invasion]," as Herodotus reports.[27] This suggests that the second burning may have been more widespread and methodical than that of the previous year. This seems entirely likely. What reason would Mardonius have had for holding back? It was the only way he could justify his march from Thessaly, and it would have helped ease the frustration that had been building up in his army, compounded by the defeat at Salamis. Even so, it is doubtful whether we should take Herodotus entirely at his word. Thucydides provides the detail that "only parts of the circumference wall were left standing and most of the houses were destroyed."[28] So, however widespread and methodical, the destruction was not total.

Before he left Attica he marched to Eleusis, some thirteen miles to the west of Athens, home of the Eleusinian Mysteries. There he ordered his men to destroy the *anaktoron* (literal meaning "palace") in the center of the Hall of Initiation.[29] Eleusis was second only to the Acropolis in sanctity. Its fame was such that it attracted initiates from all over the Greek world, making it the foremost of all the Greek mystery cults—cults, that is, that offered a salvific revelation guaranteeing blessedness in the hereafter. Mardonius could now take dubious pride in the fact that he had caused almost as much offense to Athenian—and, perhaps more importantly, Greek—religious sensibilities as his superior had done before him. Did that seem an achievement of sorts?

The Persians Withdraw from Greece

Mardonius stayed in Attica roughly a month, about the same length of time as Xerxes had done the previous year. His objective in despoiling the city and its territory was not simply to demoralize the inhabitants. He also deprived the advancing Peloponnesian army of food supplies, which had difficulty feeding itself, as it moved north into hostile territory in Boeotia.[30] It's doubtful, however, whether there was much loot to be had. Anything of value had been already filched the first time round.

After destroying Eleusis, Mardonius marched north into Boeotia, a region more suitable than Attica for a cavalry engagement, which is what he hoped to undertake. The Peloponnesians, under the command of the Spartan Pausanias, regent for the underage son of Leonidas I who died at Thermopylae, joined up with the Athenians at Eleusis. They had never intended to defend Attica, any more than they had intended to do so at the time of Xerxes' invasion. The combined force, about forty thousand in all, perhaps more, then marched north to meet Mardonius at Plataea in southern Boeotia. It was one of the largest Greek armies every assembled. It included eight thousand Athenian hoplites. The

Athenian fleet meanwhile had been placed under the command of Xanthippus, the father of Pericles.

According to tradition it was shortly before the Battle of Plataea that the Greeks took a solemn oath not to rebuild the temples that had been destroyed by the Persians. The wording of the oath as preserved by the fourth-century Athenian orator and politician Lycurgus was as follows:[31] "I will rebuild none of the shrines that have been burned and destroyed by the Persians, but I will permit them to remain as a memorial to the impiety of the barbarians to future generations." The oath is deeply problematic. The historian Theopompus of Chios, who lived in the fourth century, denounced it as an Athenian forgery, and many have followed his lead.[32] Most recently, Paul Cartledge has rejected it on the grounds that it is "an emblem . . . of what the Athenians of the later fourth century BCE wanted to believe and to convince others had been the case in 479."[33] It is also worth noting, as Peter Siewert has pointed out, that only five of the thirty-one states whose names are preserved on the Serpent Column at Delphi listing those who fought at Plataea experienced the destruction of temples firsthand, namely Athens, Eretria, Megara, Plataea, and Thespiae.[34]

As with so many contentious issues in ancient (not to mention recent) history, we will probably never know the truth, as there are compelling arguments on both sides. Though warfare in the Greek world could be extremely brutal, certain rules were generally adhered to. This included showing respect to one's own and the enemy's shrines and graves—known collectively as the "holy places"—and permitting the defeated to return to the battlefield to dispose of their dead. It was the destruction of the holy places that especially characterized the Persians as barbarians. The Oath of Plataea, taken in the immediate aftermath to the sacrilege and endorsed by the whole coalition, would have articulated and confirmed the collective sense of outrage.[35] More than that, it would have served as a permanent reminder not only of the sacrilege itself but also of those who laid down their lives in defense of freedom. It might also have been seen as a defiant response to Xerxes' instruction to Mardonius to "rebuild all the holy places I burned down."

The doubts, first raised in antiquity, are, however, disturbing. Herodotus makes no mention of the oath, which is highly problematic, since it would have functioned as an important indicator of the collective spirit of the allies before the Battle of Plataea.[36] Furthermore, the suggestion that the Athenians living in the late fourth century invented the oath in order to portray their ancestors in a flattering light has considerable merit. The refusal to eliminate the evidence of Persian barbarity was proof of the patriotic spirit of those who sacrificed everything for the survival of their *polis*, even though a generation later the Athenians would break the oath by inaugurating a massive building program on the Acropolis (see chapter 5).

The Greeks took up a position on the slopes of Mount Cithaeron, a mountain range that divides Attica from Boeotia, opposite the Persians, who established their camp on a plain on the far side of the River Asopus, where the terrain was favorable to their cavalry. The Persian army was much larger than the one that fought at Thermopylae, since it included many thousands of Theban infantry and Thessalian cavalry.[37] For ten days or more, neither side gained the advantage. Eventually, however, the Greeks no longer had a sufficient supply of water as the Persians had befouled the springs from which they had been drinking. Pausanias therefore ordered a night withdrawal, hoping to draw closer to the town of Plataea, which had a plentiful supply of water and food. Since the order caused confusion among the allies, however, Mardonius ordered an immediate attack. The Spartans and the Tegeans had to fight the Persians more or less singlehandedly, while the Athenians faced the Thebans and Thessalians.

What ultimately turned the encounter between the Persians and the Spartans in favor of the Spartans was the death of Mardonius, which caused widespread panic. The outcomes of battles in antiquity depended disproportionately on the courage and prowess of those who led their men into battle. What became of Mardonius's corpse is unknown. Herodotus reports that it disappeared the day after the battle. It was due to the Athenians that the walled camp of the Persians was successfully stormed, which the Spartans on their own had allegedly been unable to accomplish.[38] The armies of Elis and Mantinea were too late to join the battle, perhaps because they suspected the Persians would win.[39]

Artabazos, Mardonius's replacement, now abandoned any thought of further conquest and returned to the Hellespont and western Anatolia. After dedicating one-tenth of their spoils to the gods, the Greeks apportioned the remainder of their plunder among themselves. Observing how the Persians lived, Pausanias ordered his cooks to prepare a magnificent banquet for his fellow commanders using all the gold and silver and embroidered coverlets that the enemy had left behind and to set beside it a simple Spartan meal consisting of black gruel. Then he contemptuously observed, "I wanted to show you how foolish the leader of the Medes is. This is what his lifestyle was, and yet he came here to rob us of our wretched poverty."[40] Alluding to the Great King as merely the "leader of the Medes" was a deliberate insult. True or not, the anecdote says much about the Greek perception of the Persians.

The menace that had hung over Greece had finally receded, though peace would not be ratified for thirty years. On the very same day as the Battle of Plataea, so Herodotus claims, the Greek fleet put in at Mycale opposite Samos and won a victory over the Persians on their home turf.[41]

Déjà Vu

News of the victory at Plataea reached the refugees on Salamis within a few hours at the latest. It is possible a report reached them instantly via fire beacons. It took rather longer to reach Aegina and Troezen, though by nightfall it had spread throughout the Peloponnese and was making its way across the Aegean. Not only those on Salamis but also those who had been conveyed to Aegina and Troezen could now be repatriated. We don't know in what order the evacuees arrived back in Attica, but it would have made sense to leave the children in Troezen till the very last so that they could properly be cared for on their return. Once again this was an undertaking of mammoth proportions, involving the entire Athenian fleet, now reduced in size by the losses at Salamis. Indeed, the combined allied fleet according to Herodotus amounted to only 110 ships.[42] So the refugees disembarked in Attica and began the long trek home on foot.

This second homecoming must have put an even greater strain on the state's resources than the first. What provisions were available? The toll that it took on the collective psyche of the Athenian people, who had to live through this nightmare again, must have been considerable. Sights that had scarred them less than a year ago presented themselves to their gaze a second time. Some, having scrambled to rebuild their homes after the first invasion on Themistocles' recommendation, returned to find them burned down a second time, while others whose homes had escaped the violence of Xerxes' men found they had been torched by Mardonius. Tens of thousands were homeless and needing to be fed, and within two months winter would be upon them. Tens of thousands, especially slaves, were probably undernourished, if not starving. Athens's councilors and magistrates faced a daunting challenge.

A particularly pressing problem was the matter of Athens's security. Now that the Persians had departed, the Greek coalition no longer had any reason to exist—at least on the mainland. This meant that all the deep-seated rivalries that habitually divided Greek states from one another, symbolized as we saw earlier by the word *phthonos*, meaning "grudge," would immediately reassert themselves. So the camaraderie that had loosely held them together now melted like snow at Easter.

The Athenians in particular had every reason to be fearful of the Spartans, who saw them as rivals to their hegemony. The city with its fortifications laid flat was extremely vulnerable. They could, therefore, on slight provocation expect an invasion from their erstwhile ally. Their infantry was no match for the Spartans and their allies. What to do? Themistocles had the answer. Make a virtue of necessity and ring the city with a new wall by utilizing the funerary monuments that the Persians had smashed in their trail. It would be a major undertaking but security was of the highest priority. Themistocles' proposal no doubt met with resistance from a few wealthy aristocrats who had commissioned these costly works and who regarded them as sacrosanct, but the majority swiftly overwhelmed their objections. A resolution was presumably adopted to the effect that all monuments without exception be appropriated by the state.

Once the Spartans heard about the wall, however, would they not intervene to prevent it from being built? They could argue, with justification, that a walled Athens was not in the interests of the Greeks because if the Persians chose to return and invade Attica a third time, it would give them a base from which to launch an attack on the Peloponnese. Though nobody in 479 could have known that the war had ended—after all the Persians now had an even greater justification for revenge than they'd had before—the motives of the Spartans in advancing this argument were purely self-interested, their fear of Athens becoming a military rival being paramount.

This meant that the Athenians had only a brief interval before the Spartans got wind of what they were up to and intervened to prevent them—probably a few weeks at most. Once again it was Themistocles who came up with the solution. He persuaded the Athenians to send him to Sparta on a diplomatic mission while the wall was under construction and to delay the arrival of his ambassadorial colleagues until it had been completed.

Everyone was required to contribute to the building of the wall, irrespective of social position. The bulk of the labor was obviously undertaken by men of military age, though Thucydides tells us that "wives and children" also participated. He goes on to state that the Athenians "spared no private or public building which might be of use to them but tore everything down."[43] Later he describes the appearance of the wall:[44] "It is evident even today that the construction was done hastily. The foundations are made of stones of all kinds and are not finished off but are placed in the order in which each person brought them along, and there are many monuments from tombs and stones that had been sculpted. For the circuit wall was extended in every direction and it was for that reason that they made use of everything in their haste." Given its makeshift character, given too the urgency of the operation, we might have expected that the new wall would be considerably smaller than its predecessor. As Thucydides indicates, however, the opposite was the case.

Excavations conducted by the German Archaeological Service on the west side of the city in the area of the Dipylon Gate confirm the accuracy of Thucydides' account. Sculpted stones and columns from tombs, including no doubt some monuments that had not been broken, together with whatever was left standing of houses, notably the stone socles that formed the foundations for mudbrick walls, served as the lower courses of the wall. Some of the finest examples of Archaic sculpture that have survived were used to fill gaps in the wall. On display in the Ceramicus Archaeological Museum, they include a crouching sphinx that once served as a capital on a grave shaft; a grave shaft decorated with a youth holding a staff and a running gorgon in the lower register; the head and bound fist of a boxer with cauliflower ears and broken nose; and the base for a *kouros* that is decorated with youths wrestling, youths playing a ball game, and youths with a cat and dog. Making these exquisite pieces serve the mundane purpose of a fortification wall testifies eloquently to the democratic nature of the enterprise. The upper courses were made of mudbrick, manufactured equally hastily.

Sections of the new circuit, over four miles in length and pierced by at least fifteen gates, have come to light in numerous places beneath the modern city. Though the wall was largely destroyed by the terms imposed on Athens at the end of the Peloponnesian War, the circuit was repaired—with Persian money— by the Athenian general Conon in 394. Conon supervised the refurbishment in his capacity as naval commander of King Artaxerxes II, who was now siding with the Athenians in their continuing struggle against Sparta. The fortifications remained in use until the Roman general Sulla sacked the city in 86.

The building of the wall had to take precedence over the rebuilding of homes, so many thousands of Athenians continued living as refugees in temporary shacks and tents for weeks if not months after their return. Indeed, those who resided in the countryside were presumably required to remain in Athens until the first layers of the wall were up. Though some sort of defensive wall may have been in place, say, within two or three months, it's unlikely that the task was completed in much under a year. Long before that, however, Athens was effectively secure against attack.

Another urgent task was the clearing away of all the debris on the Acropolis caused by the Persian destruction so that that the site could again function as a sanctuary.[45] The Older Parthenon was largely demolished, apart from its *opis-*

thodomos or "back room," which was repaired so that it could still serve as a storage facility for the instruments of cult. The olive-wood statue of Athena, returned from Salamis, was given housing in a makeshift shack to the northeast of the temple ruins and facing its altar.[46] It was an axiom of Greek religion that all offerings to the gods, including statues, architectural reliefs, and votive offerings, remained the property of the gods and could not be removed, despite their ruined condition. So the Athenians dug a number of pits, mainly to the south of the Parthenon, and no doubt with great reverence, and deposited there all the broken pieces of sculpture.[47] Their burial turned out to be a godsend to archaeologists, since it protected them from further destruction. Athens's loss, in other words, was archaeology's gain. There were also some old statues of Athena that were damaged by the fire, described by Pausanias as "possessing all their limbs, but rather black, and too weak to withstand a blow," which the Athenians later reerected, perhaps as an enduring memorial to Persian barbarity.[48] They also buried many items of black-figure and red-figure pottery, which the fire had destroyed.

The sculptures and other artifacts were unearthed in the second half of the nineteenth century.[49] As a result of being buried, the sculptures have survived far better than classical sculptures from the Acropolis, even preserving some of the original paintwork if they had been dedicated only shortly before the devastation. They are exhibited in the new Acropolis Museum designed by Bernard Tschumi that was opened in June 2009. The museum is situated southeast of the Acropolis, only 440 yards from the Parthenon.

We don't know how long the cleaning-up operation took or what precisely it involved, but it probably wasn't until the summer of 478 that religious activity could be fully resumed. A very somber ceremony no doubt marked its commencement. Worship on the Acropolis now took place amid the makeshift structures that had been erected where the temples had once stood. No less intensive and comprehensive was the cleanup of the Agora, which also incorporated a number of sanctuaries, as well as civic buildings, in ruins. Conducting rituals on behalf of Athens's foremost deities amid such evocative reminders of the Persian sack would have been a very emotional experience. It was important to move on, however. Kathleen Lynch detects what she calls "a post-Persian War mentality of starting over or renewal," both in the rebuilding of houses that the Persians had burned down and in the closing of private wells that they had poisoned or defiled.[50]

A few months later Themistocles introduced a proposal to resume the fortification of the port town of the Piraeus, begun in 493 and interrupted by the

war. When the work had commenced, he held the position of *archōn* or magistrate. Now he was a private citizen. Thucydides believed that Themistocles was
the first to appreciate that the Piraeus with its three natural harbors offered an
unrivaled location for the home of Athens's fleet. The fortification probably took
two to three years to complete.[51] Eventually some semblance of normality returned. The Athenians were able to rebuild their homes and plant their crops,
and the familiar rhythm of daily life reestablished itself.

As for the Persians, they probably returned home without quite the same
swagger and spring in their step as when they had set out. On arrival in Sardis,
most of them probably disbanded, though Xerxes may have maintained some
military forces in western Anatolia.[52] Others presumably had to make the long
trek back to Susa and points further east, if indeed, as Herodotus claims, he had
"searched all the land of the continent" for conscripts.[53] Those from Bactria and
Sogdiana had traversed more than four thousand miles in the course of the campaign. And when the veterans finally made it back to their villages and towns,
what reception did they receive? Were any victory parades held? What stories
did they tell of their exploits? Did they confine themselves largely to talking up
their great victory at Thermopylae and of reducing Athens to rubble? What indeed was the Persian version?

Their relatives had heard no word of them since the summer or fall of 481.
We can well imagine the anxiety of those who waited for their loved ones day
after day, until the painful truth was borne by rumor in the absence of any official death tally.[54] And what did Xerxes make of it all? I hardly think he would
have shed many tears over Mardonius. Dead and defeated, his cousin had use-
fully absolved him of a large part of the blame for the expedition's failure.

-V-
The Postwar Period

Not Learning Lessons

There were, of course, important lessons to be learned from the war—lessons, it seems, that neither side learned. We'll begin with the Persians. One fact put the Persians at a distinct disadvantage: the buck did not stop at the king. After all, "military catastrophe brought no reproach upon the Achaemenid king himself."[1] On the contrary, the buck stopped with those under his immediate command.

We can be confident that when Xerxes returned to his capital at Susa, he did not conduct a post mortem. That would have led him and his immediate circle to the embarrassing conclusion that the autocratic style of military leadership had contributed significantly to the outcome. As a result of dallying at the Hellespont and at Doriscus, and as a result, too, of treating his invasion as a royal progress, he had arrived in Attica only when the campaigning season was drawing to a close. He had allowed himself to be fooled by Themistocles. He had withdrawn his land army at the moment when he might have faced and overcome the Peloponnesians.

Even so, the view presented in Aeschylus's *Persians* that Xerxes had suffered a catastrophic reversal with profound consequences for the Persian

Empire, which now went into irreversible decline, has no basis in fact, not least because the empire endured for another 150 years. The Greek mercenary officer and historian Xenophon, writing at the very end of the fifth century, puts the following comment into the mouth of Cyrus the Younger:[2] "Gentlemen, my father's empire stretches to the south where people cannot live because of the heat and to the north where they cannot live because of the cold. And all that lies in between is held by my brother's friends, who are satraps." Though this is, of course, a wild exaggeration, it nonetheless indicates that the impression of Persian greatness was not terminally dented by Xerxes. Once we rid ourselves of that interpretation, the hard question is that posed by Pierre Briant: "What is the significance of the year 479 in Persian history?"[3] So, too, Amélie Kuhrt has warned of the dangers of "letting a setback suffered in one campaign along the empire's north-western fringe define an entire reign of twenty-one years."[4]

Highly instructive is the Persian version of the Greco-Persian Wars, which Dio Chrysostom of Prusa, a rhetorician who lived from circa 40 to 120 CE, preserves. It is similar in tone to the poem by Robert Graves quoted in chapter 1.[5]

> I heard a Mede state that the Persians do not admit any of the claims made by the Greeks. Instead they say that Darius sent forces under Datis and Artaphernes against Naxos and Euboea, and that when they had captured these cities, they returned to the King. However, while they were lying off Euboea, a few of their ships, not more than twenty, were driven to Attica and their sailors had a battle of sorts with the people who lived there. Afterward Xerxes, who was leading an expedition against Greece, defeated the Spartans at Thermopylae and killed Leonidas their king. He then took and destroyed Athens and enslaved all those who did not escape. Following this, he imposed a tribute on the Greeks and returned to Asia.

According to Dio Chrysostom in other words, Xerxes fed his subjects a big fat Persian lie. As a result, they had only a vague sense of what happened at Marathon and knew nothing at all about Salamis. Dio ends with this comment: "It is obvious that this version (i.e., the Mede's description of the Greco-Persian Wars) is false, and it is quite likely—because, after all, this would be the natural thing to do—that the King gave the order that it be circulated among the tribes that lived inland so that they should not become restive." It is salutary to reflect upon the degree to which truth has throughout history lost out to propaganda, though the irony here is that Dio's own report of the Persian version is almost certainly false as well.

The defeat at the hands of the Greeks must have rankled Xerxes, however, no matter what public face he put upon it, because around 467 he began mustering a large fleet at the mouth of the Eurymedon River, just off the coast of southern Turkey. It was perhaps his intention to reconquer Thrace, or at least that part of Ionia, which was now under Athenian control. While his ships were still gathering, however, a Greek fleet under the command of the Athenian admiral Cimon took them by surprise and delivered a crippling blow. The Greeks disembarked and defeated the Persians on land. Never again would a Persian expedition invade Greece. Yet despite the victory, things did not go entirely Athens's way. Probably soon after the battle the Athenians suffered a serious defeat in Thrace, while the Persians immediately rebuilt their navy.[6]

In July or August 465, fate, the gods, or his evil destiny finally caught up with Xerxes. Or so pious and vindictive Greeks believed. The details are obscure, but Greek sources claim that the eunuch in charge of the imperial bedchamber and the captain of the royal guard jointly carried out Xerxes' assassination and that of the crown prince Datis, perhaps on behalf of Xerxes' third son, who now became Artaxerxes I.[7] There is no report of Xerxes' death in any Persian source except for a Babylonian astronomical tablet, which merely states that Xerxes was killed by his son.[8] The news would have taken several days to reach Athens, brought perhaps by a merchant vessel that docked in the Piraeus. No doubt there were many who cheered heartily when they heard it, while the majority in Persia may well have been grief-stricken.[9]

The Athenians, however, were no more self-critical than Xerxes. Victors are rarely inclined to ask tough questions, and it wasn't in their interest to eat humble pie. They seem to have ignored the fact that they could so easily have lost the war and that so many accidental factors had contributed to their success, even though, to their credit, they had displayed nerves of steel. The way they saw it, the gods had been on their side. They made this idea palpable by commissioning the Athenian sculptor Phidias, who later worked on the Parthenon sculptures and later still on the statue of Olympian Zeus at Olympia, to carve a statue of the goddess Nemesis (Retribution). Nemesis was one of several personifications whom the Greek deified and worshiped. Phidias made use of a block of Parian marble—marble, that is from the Cycladic island of Paros—that the Persians had brought with them in 490, "in order to make a trophy out of it as if they had already succeeded, arrogantly thinking that nothing prevented them from seizing Athens," as Pausanias caustically writes.[10] Appropriately the sculpture was set up in the goddess's temple at Rhamnous, whose predecessor the Persian fleet had burned on its way from Artemisium to Phaleron.

The belief that the gods had punished Xerxes for what the Greeks called *hubris*—"insolence" or "wanton violence"—was widely endorsed at the time.[11] It features prominently in Aeschylus's *Persians*, as we shall see. Herodotus, too, who drew heavily from Aeschylus for book 8 of his *History*, subscribed to it. He puts the following pious words into the mouth of Themistocles, when the latter is giving his assessment of the victory at Salamis. Whether Themistocles actually delivered these words or something similar is another matter altogether:[12] "It wasn't we who achieved this success but the gods and the heroes, because they begrudged the fact that one man who was unholy and rash should rule over Asia and Europe. He was indifferent to the distinction between things that are holy and things that are profane, burning and toppling over the statues of the gods. He even scourged the sea and threw shackles into it."

If you'd been in the Athenian Agora in the months following the Persian withdrawal, you would have witnessed a great deal of self-congratulatory backslapping. Most Athenians subscribed to the belief that it was their moral superiority over the slavish and effeminate barbarians that had secured their victory. Was there no one prepared to look facts in the face? Herodotus for one wasn't blind to Athens's shortcomings. The last incident he describes involves what we would consider to be a war crime. Having imprisoned Artaÿktes, the Persian governor of Sestos in the Thracian Chersonese, for committing an act of sacrilege in the shrine of the hero Protesilaus, the Athenians nailed him to a plank and stoned his son to death before his eyes.[13]

Herodotus's principal narrative ends with the return of the Persians to Asia. In 479, of course, the Greeks didn't know that the enemy was gone for good, since there was now all the more reason for them to seek vengeance. Over time, however, the defeat of the barbarians came to be regarded as "the supremely Greek achievement," as Peter Rhodes observed, irrespective of the fact that not all states had joined the coalition.[14] A few Greeks, less invested in why the Athenians had survived than the Athenians themselves, were able to recognize how narrowly they had escaped defeat. Thucydides reports that a Corinthian ambassador who was sent to Sparta just before the outbreak of the Peloponnesian War half a century later claimed that the Persians had failed because of the strategic errors they had committed, though admittedly the reason he does so is to undermine the Athenian boast that it was they who were the saviors of Greece.[15] No doubt many Greeks were sick to their back teeth, constantly hearing this claim trotted out. The boast was nonetheless understandable. The Athenians had been terrorized by the Persians. So they instigated a curse on anyone who suggested making peace with the Persians that was recited at the opening of every meeting of the Assembly. It remained in effect until the fourth century BCE.[16]

The Greeks did not change their modus operandi as a result of the war. On the contrary, they quickly reverted to their habit of interminable internecine squabbling, which often led to the massacre of their fellow Greeks. Interstate dynamics were, moreover, largely unaffected by the outcome of the war. States that had medized were not punished, while those that had remained loyal gained little benefit.

There was, however, one conspicuous exception. That one exception was Athens, which, as Robin Osborne notes, drew this sinister lesson from the war, namely "that a cause"—that is, that of safeguarding the Greeks against the Persians—"which exerted moral pressure on cities could be used to render those cities subject, in the name of liberty."[17] Immediately after the Greeks had defeated the Persians at the Battle of Mycale, the Athenians, with the acquiescence of Sparta, founded a naval alliance, whose objective according to Thucydides was to ravage and plunder Persian territory, though it certainly had the additional aim of protecting the Ionian cities and islands from Persian aggression and of preventing the Persians from launching another attack on the mainland.[18] Over the course of the next fifty years the Athenians came to acquire undisputed dominance over the Aegean and its littoral by converting their alliance into an empire. And once the threat of Persia had been removed, possibly after the conclusion of peace in either 465/4 or 450/49, the Athenians did not politely stand down and declare mission accomplished. Instead, they used the surplus from the tribute money that they exacted from their allies to increase the size of their navy and finance a costly rebuilding program. In effect the Athenians, at the head of the Delian Confederacy, so named by modern scholars because its treasury was on the sacred island of Delos, proved themselves fully Xerxes' equal in *folie de grandeur*, and indeed his apt pupil, though it is doubtful whether any of them appreciated the irony. Herodotus, however, certainly did.

There was one positive consequence from the war, though it can hardly go under the heading of a lesson that was learned, given the fact that it was unlearned soon afterward. The Athenian state might have tottered, but it had hung together, and the citizen body probably found itself more unified at the end of the war than it had ever been before, not least because rich and poor had served alongside one another, even in some cases no doubt on the same rowing bench. More than that, the rich had made a disproportionate sacrifice to the common good because it was their estates that had been the principal victim of Persian vengeance.

Even so, I seriously doubt whether this newfound solidarity, this peace dividend as we might call it, lasted more than a few years, or that it extended to the slaves who had made a signal contribution to the victory at Salamis. It would be gratifying to think that the Athenians had the good grace to free those who had served as rowers, but given the fact that a fair percentage of the slave workforce had probably used the opportunity to escape, it is likely the citizenry faced a demographic servile shortfall that put paid to any humanitarian consideration. The shortfall was all the more critical in light of the fact that the economy was in tatters, the countryside burned, the housing situation dire, food supplies limited, and that they needed every available pair of hands to repair the devastation. It's possible that the Athenians acquired Persian slaves as a result of the victory at Plataea, but if so we hear nothing of it.

Thanking the Gods

We tend to think of fifth-century Greece as an age of rationalism and, in so doing, are liable to overlook the fact that the Greeks consistently ascribed victory in battle to their gods. Belief in divine intervention permeates Herodotus's account of the Greco-Persian Wars, and probably most Greeks believed that they would not have withstood and eventually overcome the Persian threat if the gods and the heroes had not fought alongside them. The Delphic Oracle had given sound, if ambiguous, advice. Divine Salamis had indeed brought death to the sons of (Persian) women.

It has been suggested that the most spectacular thank offering for the victory was the Temple of Zeus at Olympia, which was built between 472 and 458 at the latest. Its west pediment depicts a Centauromachy, a struggle between half-man and half-horse centaurs and Lapiths, that is to say, between a lower order of being and a higher order, which might have been intended to symbolize the struggle between the Persians and the Greeks. Whether it symbolized the struggle or not, the fact remains that Olympia was the most important sanctuary for the member states of the Peloponnesian League. As Richard Tomlinson points out, therefore, "It would be natural to expect to find there tangible evidence of monuments constructed to commemorate the Greek victory."[19]

In acknowledgment of its own indebtedness to the gods, the Athenian *dēmos* took the decision to upgrade several existing cults and introduce new ones. By "introduce" I mean pass a motion permitting the worship of a deity who, up to that point, had not been formally admitted into the Athenian pantheon. Greek

Apollo presiding over the battle between Lapiths and centaurs, west pediment at Olympia

religion was a civic affair, and the worship of the gods was in the control of the state.

Pan, who had not only assisted the Athenians at Marathon but also intervened at Salamis, was awarded his long-awaited niche or cave on the northwest slope of the Acropolis. That might seem a poor recompense for his contribution to the victory at Marathon—it was he allegedly who had caused the Persians to "panic"—but being an agricultural deity of humble origins who was partly animal, he was not accepted on Olympus, where the principal gods resided. For this reason, no temple was ever erected in his honor. Athens wasn't the only site of his worship in Attica. On the contrary, the cult of Pan became widespread throughout the territory, though in some caves he had a presence before the Persian War period.[20] The Athenian general Miltiades, who was largely responsible for the victory at Marathon, dedicated a statue to the god at Marathon, which bore the following epigram:[21] "Miltiades erected me, Pan, the goat-footed, the Arcadian, the enemy of the/Medes, the friend of the Athenians."

Another deity who was accepted into the Athenian pantheon at this time was Boreas, the personification of the north wind. Boreas was accorded this honor because when the Athenians prayed to him before the Battle of Artemisium, he had sent a gale that had allegedly wrecked four hundred Persian ships, thereby narrowing the odds in favor of the Greeks considerably. The Athenians established his cult by the banks of the River Ilissus, at the spot where he was believed to have abducted an Athenian princess called Oreithyia.[22]

Artemis Mounychia, who already owned an imposing sanctuary on Mounychia Hill overlooking Salamis, was honored with a prestigious festival because "the goddess shone as a full moon upon the Greeks as they were conquering at Salamis."[23] Though it's unclear how the full moon contributed to the victory, it's possible that its light had enabled the Greeks to obtain information regarding the disposition of the Persian fleet on the night before the battle.

Special games were instituted in honor of Heracles, since the Athenians had encamped in his sanctuary at Marathon before the battle was fought. The inhabitants of Marathon claimed they were the first people to worship Heracles as a god. They no doubt lobbied for his elevation, which brought considerable distinction to their deme.[24]

The Athenians dedicated an imposing stoa to Zeus Eleutherios (Liberator) on the west side of the Agora just south of the Royal Stoa. The epithet Eleutherios referred to the fact that the god had enabled the Greeks to achieve freedom as a result of their victory at Plataea. A stoa is a civic building in the form of a colonnade. This one had projecting wings on either end. Though it wasn't built until circa 430, the god was probably being worshiped on the site much earlier, perhaps as soon as the war ended. But even if he wasn't, the introduction of the new cult half a century later testifies to what Robert Parker has described as "the unique intensity with which the national crisis and triumph were experienced."[25]

At an unknown site in Athens, possibly soon after the war had ended, the Athenians erected a Temple of Eukleia (Glory), which Pausanias describes as "a dedication from the Medes who landed at Marathon."[26] Other cults that were introduced or promoted as a result of the Greco-Persian Wars include those of Artemis Agrotera, Theseus, and Zeus Tropaios. It's also likely that the Attic silver tetradrachma (coin worth four drachmae) that was introduced in the second half of the fifth century depicting Athena wearing a helmet with three olive leaves commemorates the victory at Salamis.

Themistocles took it upon himself to immortalize the naval victory by financing a sanctuary to Artemis Aristoboule (Of the Brilliant Counsel) in the deme of Melite, of which he was a member, just west of modern-day Theseus Square in downtown Athens. Plutarch tells us that he gave Artemis the epithet Aristoboule "on the grounds that he"—note the presumptuous use of the masculine pronoun—"had given absolutely brilliant counsel to the *polis* and to the Greeks."[27]

Silver tetradrachma from Athens, second half of fifth century

Though Plutarch does not specify at this point what Themistocles' brilliant counsel was, he indicates elsewhere that it was connected with the decision to fight at Salamis. It was, of course, equally due to Themistocles' "brilliant counsel" that two years earlier the Athenians had put the wealth that accrued to them from their silver strike at Laurium into building a fleet, without which they would have been sunk, metaphorically speaking. It was thus entirely fitting, in his eyes at least, to acknowledge the divinely inspired monition, twice rendered to him, that had saved Athens from abject servitude.[28] Themistocles also "repaired and adorned with paintings" at his own cost the Initiation Hall at Eleusis that the Persians had burned down. He did so in violation of the Oath of Plataea, if indeed such an oath was taken.[29] The hall in question had originally been paid for by the Lycomid *genos* (or "noble kin-group") to which Themistocles himself belonged, so he probably undertook its repair as much to bolster his family pride as to demonstrate his benevolence and patriotism.

The sole memorial to the evacuation itself of which we have record stood in Troezen. In a colonnade inside the agora, as Pausanias tells us, stone statues, described as "likenesses," were set up of the women and children "whom the

Athenians had given to the Troezenians to preserve." Unfortunately, Pausanias does not tell us what material the statues were made of or how many figures were depicted, so we are in no position to judge how imposing it was. However, the fact that it was a group portrait is in itself impressive. Pausanias does, however, reveal that there were "not many" statues and that they were all of "women of note." It would be fascinating to know whether the Athenians or the Troezenians had taken the initiative to set up the monument.[30] Might it conceivably have been a gift of the Athenian people to their hosts, paid for perhaps by the women of note themselves? Possibly the monument was erected at the same time as the so-called Decree of Themistocles, though that in turn raises the question as to why the Troezenians were celebrating an event that had occurred a century and a half earlier at this particular moment.

Whatever it was that prompted the erection of the monument, it was presumably intended to serve as a reminder of the close and abiding ties that existed between the two communities. The fact that the monument survived for six hundred years in such a prominent location is a testimony to the importance of the event in the collective memory. This is all the more remarkable in light of what happened less than twenty years after the war had ended. Their indebtedness to the Troezenians did not prevent the Athenians from attacking and occupying their city either during the so-called First Peloponnesian War that was fought between Athens and Corinth (c. 461) or in the Second or Main Peloponnesian War that broke out in 431. We might at least hope that the occupation was conducted with some civility. Pausanias tells us he also saw an altar to Helios Eleutherios (Sun of Freedom), which the Troezenians erected "after escaping enslavement by Xerxes and the Persians."[31]

The Aeginetans had even more cause to rue the day they had given refuge to their former enemy. In 458/7 the Athenians forcibly incorporated them into their empire and ordered them to pay a punitive annual tribute of thirty talents. In 431 they evicted the Aeginetans en masse from their island, alleging that they were "chiefly responsible" for the Peloponnesian War.[32]

Eclipsing Pausanias and Themistocles

"There was not one great Greek general in the entire history of the city-state . . . who was not at some time either fined, exiled, or demoted, or killed alongside his troops," Victor Hanson points out.[33] High visibility aroused enmity in the ancient world, and the Spartan regent Pausanias and the Athenian naval commander Themistocles were no exceptions to the rule. When less than a decade after Plataea Pausanias found himself accused of plotting to overthrow the Spartan state by offering citizenship to helot rebels and of medizing, he took refuge in the sanctuary of Athena Chalkioikos or "Brazen House," so named because the statue of the goddess stood in a brazen shrine. Immured inside the sanctuary, he was on the point of dying of starvation, whereupon he was dragged outside so that his corpse should not be a source of pollution.

Themistocles was ostracized and sent into exile in 472 or 471, less than a decade after the victory at Salamis. Even before the Battle of Plataea he seems to have become a highly controversial figure, as we saw earlier, and the fact that he ascribed the victory at Salamis in large part to the luminosity of his intellect can only have further rankled his compatriots.[34] Yet another reason for his unpopularity was a dispute as to whether Athens's salvation was due primarily to the infantry victory at Marathon or to the naval victory at Salamis—a dispute that he seems to have lost. Matters cannot have been helped by the fact that he and Cimon, the son of Miltiades, who had been chiefly responsible for the victory at Marathon, were bitter political rivals.

Later, when Themistocles had been sent into exile, the Spartans accused him of conspiring with the Persians.[35] Plutarch says that he likened himself to a plane tree, which the Athenians took shelter under when a storm was brewing, but whose branches they lopped off when fair weather prevailed.[36] Themistocles was condemned to death in absentia and hunted down like a common criminal. He eventually fled to the court of King Artaxerxes I, Xerxes' successor. Artaxerxes received Themistocles hospitably, and in time the Athenian came to be held "in higher honor than any Greek before or since," as Thucydides states,[37] serving as the governor of Magnesia on the Maeander River. There he resided until his death, which probably came about as the result of natural causes. He was in his mid-sixties.

He remained at heart an Athenian, however. His friends, in accordance with his wishes, repatriated his bones secretly, it being forbidden to bury an outlaw who had been condemned to death for treason in Attic soil. An unfluted column within a square enclosure, restored in 1952, appropriately situated at the southwest extremity of the Piraeus peninsula and overlooking Salamis, is said to mark his tomb.[38] As Robert Lenardon has aptly observed, an appropriate moment to rehabilitate his memory by means of a prominently placed memorial would have been circa 395, when the Athenians took the decision to rebuild the Piraeus fortifications that had been destroyed at the end of the Peloponnesian

War.[39] Later still, a statue of Themistocles was set up in the Theater of Dionysus, alongside those of the three canonical tragedians, Aeschylus, Sophocles,
and Euripides.[40]

Rebuilding Athens

The priority at the end of the war was to fortify Athens against the possibility of a Spartan invasion. Only after the so-called Themistoclean Wall had been
built did the Athenians have the leisure to rebuild their homes. Did the same
corporate spirit that the population had demonstrated before now extend to
this enterprise? For those who were childless and elderly, it would have been a
daunting, if not impossible, undertaking.

One of the few civic undertakings in the immediate aftermath to the war was
the building of a retaining wall around the north side of the Acropolis. The wall
incorporated fragments of architraves, cornices, and a frieze from the sixth
century temple, along with a number of unfluted column drums from the Older
Parthenon that were inserted into the upper wall. Their prominent display
served as a perpetual reminder of the sack, even when decades later all other
evidence of it had been erased.

In addition, a round building with a conical roof known as the Tholos was
built on the west side of the Agora. It was here that the fifty members from each
of the ten tribes that composed the Boulē were fed at public expense for the
thirty-five or thirty-six days when they served as *prytaneis* or "presidents." Sometime between 475 and 450 the Stoa Poikilē or Painted Colonnade was constructed
on the north side of the Agora. It was so named because it was decorated with
paintings on large wooden panels, including one depicting the Battle of Marathon, by Athens's leading artists.[41]

In the mid-450s the Athenians erected a colossal bronze statue of Athena
on the Acropolis. Executed by Phidias and known in later times as Athena Promachos (i.e., "She who fights in the front rank"), it commemorated either the
Battle of Marathon or the Greco-Persian Wars in general. From Pausanias's
claim that the tip of Athena's spear and the crest of her helmet were visible to
sailors some fifty miles away at Cape Sunium, it is estimated that the statue
stood over thirty-six feet high.[42] For nearly a decade Athena Promachos tow-
ered over the Acropolis without any rival until the building of the Parthenon,
whose roof was nearly ten feet higher. The statue stood on the Acropolis for
about one thousand years until 465 CE when it was removed to Constantinople
by the Byzantines. It was melted down in the early thirteenth century, alleg-

edly by a superstitious mob that believed the goddess was inviting Crusaders into their city. No traces of it have survived, except for remains of a platform surrounding the statue and depictions of the statue on coins.[43]

Restoring the Acropolis

After German bombers had destroyed Coventry Cathedral in the West Midlands of England on the night of November 14, 1940, the decision was taken to leave the ruined shell "as a moving reminder of the folly and waste of war," to inscribe the words "Father, forgive" on the wall behind the altar, and to build a new cathedral beside it. The Kaiser Wilhelm Memorial Church in Berlin, destroyed by allied bombing, has also been kept as a ruin and a newer church built beside it.

The Athenian *dēmos* did not see fit to repair the buildings on the Acropolis immediately, though not "as a moving reminder of the folly and waste of war"— that was not an idea Greeks would have understood even remotely. Nor was it because Athens was financially impoverished by the wars. On the contrary, the plunder taken from the Persians after Plataea and the victories secured in the years following, culminating in Cimon's victory at the River Eurymedon around 466, were a source of considerable enrichment to the Athenians. Instead, it is likely that the buildings were left in their ruined state in memory of the barbarism of the enemy. Whether their decision was the result of an oath that they and other Greeks took at the Battle of Plataea is, as we have seen, still debated.

A generation would pass before the Athenians decided to restore the Acropolis to its former glory—or, rather, to restore it in such a way that it would far exceed its former glory. In the interim, however, it must have been extremely moving to conduct religious ceremonies amid the debris. The ruined Acropolis, flattened and blackened, thus served as a record of hate.

The Athenians were not alone in memorializing ruined buildings. The Phocians preserved the Temple of Apollo at Abae as a ruin as well.[44] Other cities that had been on the path of Xerxes' invasion might later claim that they had suffered devastation in order to add luster to their fame. As John Boardman notes, any collapsed building could be identified as the work of the Persians, whereas in reality it might simply have been a ruin.[45]

By 448, however, the situation had changed. A new generation had matured, and with it a need for renewal had emerged. It was in fact those who had been impressionable adolescents at the time of the destruction who now, about thirty years later, assumed responsibility. Athens, an imperial power in its own right, now the most powerful state in the eastern Mediterranean, was certainly not strapped for cash, being the recipient of large sums of money in the form of annual tribute from its allies. Quite likely, too, the *polis* saw itself in competition with its old enemy, Persia. So, on the initiative of a rising statesman called Pericles, the *dēmos* took the decision to rebuild. Pericles was destined to be at the helm of Athenian politics until the early years of the Peloponnesian War, and it was he, more than anyone else, who gave Athens's golden era its distinctive character. The decision may have followed upon the concluding of the so-called Peace of Callias with Persia, named for its chief negotiator.[46]

An inscription dated by its letter forms around 450 provides the earliest evidence for the decision to begin rebuilding on the Acropolis. It has to do with the construction of a new gate belonging to the Temple of Athena Nike (Victory), which was to replace the one destroyed by the Persians. The Temple of Nike is located at the southwest corner of the Acropolis, just outside the monumental gateway known as the Propylaea. In the event the proposal was not implemented, and in due course it was decided to reconstruct the whole sanctuary. The project was finished in 410 with the building of a parapet with sculptural reliefs.[47]

Perhaps it was the impulse to restore this gate that motivated the *dēmos* to draw up a master plan for the whole Acropolis. At any rate in 447 work began on a new Parthenon, which John Camp described as "a long-delayed victory monument for the epic struggle against the Persians."[48] Many scholars agree. Andrew Stewart, for instance, referring to the metopes along the outer walls that depict both Lapiths fighting centaurs and Amazons fighting Athenians, describes the subject matter as an expression of "the familiar antithesis between east and west, barbarism and civilization, and *hubris* and *nemesis*,"[49] though some scholars, such as Karim Arafat,[50] have challenged the allegorical interpretation.

The temple was built to house a new gold and ivory statue of Athena by Phidias. Like the statue of Athena Promachos, it too may have ended up in Constantinople, though in this case we are lucky to possess a miniature copy known as the Varvakeion Athena, named after its find spot in Athens. It is dated circa 200–250 CE and stands just over three feet in height. The original was about thirty-eight feet high.

While the Parthenon was still under construction, in 438 work began on the new Propylaea. The ornamental gateway would remain unfinished at the outbreak of the Peloponnesian War in 431 and was never completed. Work on the Erechtheum, the Temple of Poseidon and Erechtheus, began sometime after an uneasy peace had been concluded between Athens and Sparta in 421. The temple was completed in 406, only two years before Athens's final defeat at the hands of the Peloponnesians.

The Acropolis building project had taken more than forty years. As Richard Tomlinson states, however, "It still seems best to consider this reconstruction essentially as the achievement of a single, unified plan . . . not the haphazard adding of buildings without forethought over an interminable period."[51] As we have seen, the restoration of the Acropolis by no means obliterated all indications of the Persian sack. On the contrary, memorials of the conflagration were deliberately left visible. The use of a block of marble from the architrave of the Older Parthenon to record the list of Athens's tribute payers and the amounts each paid in the years from 454/3 to 440/39 may have been yet another reminder of how Athens had literally risen from the ashes.[52]

Writing Up Salamis

Not surprisingly the Greco-Persian Wars proved a fertile source of inspiration for poets, even as late as the third century BCE. In 476, with the financial backing of Themistocles, Phrynichus, the same tragedian who had been fined for putting on stage the *Capture of Miletus*, presented a play called the *Phoenician Women*, which dealt with Salamis and the lamentation that followed. The title derives from its chorus of widows of Phoenician sailors, who composed the majority of Xerxes' naval personnel.[53] The play begins with a eunuch announcing the defeat of Xerxes while chairs are being set out for the royal councilors.[54] It and the other three plays in the tetralogy won first prize in the dramatic competition. In 474 Pindar wrote a dithyramb, a poem in honor of the god Dionysus that was sung by a chorus of fifty, in which he eulogized the Athenians for their part in the Greco-Persian Wars. Pindar flatteringly described Athens as "gleaming, violet-crowned, famed in song, the bulwark of Greece, divine city," whose children had established "the foundations of liberty."[55] Simonides, best known for his epigrams, wrote a lyric poem and an elegy on Salamis. He also wrote several epigrams about the wars.[56]

Undoubtedly the greatest poetic work inspired by the Greco-Persian Wars is Aeschylus's *Persians*. The play was produced in 472 and is the oldest surviving example of drama in the Western repertoire. Two years later, on the invitation of the Sicilian tyrant Hieron, Aeschylus performed it in Syracuse.[57] According to the author of its *hypothesis* (a short introduction to the play written some time later), Aeschylus "modeled" his play on Phrynichus's *Phoenician Women*. The action takes place in Susa near the tomb of Darius.[58] The chorus comprises venerable Persian elders, who are councilors of the king. One of its most memorable features is the Messenger's eyewitness account of the Battle of Salamis. His speech is prefaced by the following exchange between him and Queen Atossa, the mother of Xerxes, who incidentally is not named in the play:[59]

> Messenger: The gods preserve the city of the goddess Pallas [i.e., Athena].
> Atossa: Has Athens then not been destroyed?
> Messenger: So long as there are men, there is a strong defense.

The Messenger is being economical with the truth. Very likely Aeschylus omitted even the briefest description of the burning for fear of stirring up painful memories. As Michael Gagarin notes, however, the omission may partly have been intended to exonerate Themistocles for having recommended the abandonment of Athens.[60] It was certainly not the case that the victory at Salamis had laid former political rivalries to rest. And besides, some Athenians may still have resented a policy that led to the destruction of their homes and property.

Later the Messenger evokes the moment when the Persians who are guarding the exits at the Straits of Salamis realize to their horror that they have been fooled. They are alerted to this realization by a trumpet blast, followed by bosuns' commands, from across the water:[61] "Quickly all the ships became visible to us. The right wing advanced first in perfect order, then the whole armament advanced and we heard a great shout: 'Go forward, sons of Greece, liberate your fatherland, liberate your children, your wives, the temples of your ancestral gods, and the tombs of your ancestors! The contest now is for all!'" These lines may well have aroused patriotic pride in the audience, prompting some to cheer when they heard them. Aeschylus, however, does not let his audience bask in Athens's accomplishment for long. Some twenty lines later the Messenger strikes a very different chord by describing how the victors gave free rein to their murderous instincts, once the Persians no longer had any means of defending themselves:[62]

> The enemy [i.e., the Athenians] kept striking our men and hacking at them with
> broken oars and the flotsam from the wrecked vessels just as if they were tunny
> fish or some other fish you catch in nets, so that shrieks and cries echoed over
> the deep until the eye of black night hid the scene. Not if I were to take ten days
> enumerating the full catalog of horrors could I come to the end of my account.
> Never before did so many men die in one day.

Perhaps Aeschylus intended these lines to be a reminder of what civilized people do in war. He may well have witnessed this "barbaric" (*sic*) spectacle firsthand and been sickened by it. A leading question is, Did the entire audience take pride as it heard these words, or did a few wince as they remembered their brutality?

Atossa, though devastated by the Messenger's news, is depicted as a tower of strength in the face of adversity. Xerxes by contrast comes off badly, having "hurled himself into reckless flight" after his defeat. Such is the magnitude of the catastrophe that "only a few have fled back home." "The whole of Asia groans, stripped of everything." Persia's entire armament, both navy and army, have been destroyed.[63] The empire is now on the brink of collapse, so the Chorus of Elders claims:[64] "Throughout the land of Asia for a long time to come people will no longer obey the laws of the Persians, nor pay tribute under imperial duress. No longer will they prostrate themselves in reverence as the strength of the Great King exists no more. Tongues will no longer be held in check. The people have been released and speak freely, now the yoke of repression has been removed." Wishful thinking indeed, yet calculated no doubt to raise a cheer in the audience.

To what extent Aeschylus's play is racist in tone, as has sometimes been claimed, remains to a large extent a matter of interpretation. Is the playwright suggesting that Xerxes' flaws are ones that are distinctively Persian and the consequence of the Persian political and social structure? Or is he implying that they are merely human flaws, despite the differences between the two peoples? He certainly emphasizes the superiority of Greek democracy over autocratic monarchy, but he does not vilify the Persians themselves. He indicates that Xerxes is guilty of *hubris*, but he does not condemn him utterly, though he certainly portrays him less favorably than his predecessor Darius I.[65] In fact the chorus primarily lays the blame for the disaster on the *daimōn* or "fateful spirit" that took possession of him and diseased his wits.[66] Moreover, as Christopher Tuplin has pointed out, distinctive, ethnographical references to Persians in the play are limited, perhaps most prominent being "Persian or Persian-sounding, but actually fake names," only five of which can be assigned to known commanders.[67] Tragedies inspired by the Greco-Persian Wars continued to be produced as late as the fourth and even third centuries BCE.[68]

Either at the end of the fifth century or at the beginning of the fourth, Timotheus of Miletus wrote a citharodic poem (one that was accompanied by the *cithara*, an instrument related to the lyre) about the Battle of Salamis, which was influenced by Aeschylus's play. Like Aeschylus, Timotheus presents the battle from the Persian point of view. He makes no mention of Athens, though it is thought likely that the missing part of the poem may have done so. The focus in the extant part is on the visceral experience of fighting at sea. Particularly memorable is a passage in which a drowning Persian is depicted struggling for his life. Another striking feature is the comparison of the ships to parts of the human body. For instance, when they are being rammed they are said to lose their "limbs" and reveal their "ribs."[69]

Emulating the Persians

Margaret Miller alleges, with a pinch of exaggeration, that "the claims of contempt"—that is, toward the Persians on the part of the Athenians—"are disproved by the evidence of archaeology, epigraphy, iconography, and literature, all of which reveal some facet of Athenian receptivity to Achaemenid Persian culture." But isn't it possible to admire artistry while despising the artist?[70] Cultural attitudes are, moreover, highly complex, even in the case of single individuals. When my father returned from World War II after being held a prisoner of the Japanese for three years, he could not tolerate having anything that had been made in Japan in the house, whereas he cordially received an English-speaking former prison guard, who appeared at his newsagent shop unannounced. Miller's point that the Athenians were receptive to certain aspects of Persian culture is, however, well taken. Their receptivity came about in part because they, like other Greeks, acquired plentiful booty as the result of their capture of the Persian camp at Plataea. This booty was, in Miller's words, "the single largest intrusion of Persian (and other foreign) goods into Greek society."[71]

Some Greeks, including the Spartan regent Pausanias, even adopted the Persian dress code. Slippers and the so-called sleeved *chiton*, a long-sleeved garment worn by both men and women, became popular in certain circles. It is likely, however, that some odium attached to those who cultivated a penchant for things Persian. Of the seven hundred *ostraka* dated to the mid-480s that are inscribed with the name of Callias, son of Cratius, sixteen accuse him of medizing.[72] This is not a big number, but it reflects suspicion toward someone who was judged to be too thick with "the enemy," particularly as one *ostrakon* depicts him dressed as a Persian. Another derisively accuses the politician Aristides of being "the brother of Datis the Mede," one of the two commanders of the Persian army at the Battle of Marathon. As the decades passed, the taste for Persian extravagance had to compete with the fad for Spartan austerity.

Plutarch reports the tradition that the so-called Odeion (literally "the place of odes or poetry"), which the Athenians erected to the east of the Theater of Dionysus in the 440s or 430s "with many seats and many columns," was intended to replicate Xerxes' tent, abandoned after Plataea, that had been awarded to the Athenians for their valor in battle. But it is also possible that its design was inspired by the audience hall known as the Apadana at Persepolis, from which the Great King watched ceremonies held in the courtyards.[73] The Parthenon frieze was almost certainly inspired by the Apadana reliefs as well, as Margaret Root has demonstrated, though the Persepolis reliefs may in turn be the work of Ionian Greek artists.[74]

By drawing inspiration from Persian architecture in the construction and elaboration of such prominent buildings, the Athenians were surely seeking to place themselves on an equal imperial footing with the Persians.[75] They were not alone in commemorating their victory architecturally. The Spartans, too, erected in their agora what they called the Persian Stoa, which they paid for from the spoils of victory. The colonnaded building was enlarged over time and included marble statues of both Mardonius, the Persian general, and Artemisia, the queen of Halicarnassus who fought on the Persian side.[76]

Stereotyping the Barbarian

There are indications that the stereotype of the "barbarian" was already beginning to take shape in the Greek mindset as early as the seventh century BCE. Homer refers to a *barbarophōnos* or "barbarian-speaking" Carian called Nastes, who wears gold "like a girl" and who is "childishly stupid." Such characteristics—incapacity to speak Greek properly, ostentatiousness, and effeminacy—are later attributed to barbarians in general.[77] The word *barbaros*, however, meaning "of non-Greek speech," does not appear in Homer and is rarely attested until the period of the Greco-Persian Wars. In Aeschylus's *Persians* and in Herodotus's *Histories*, it is applied to all non-Greeks, partly no doubt because the invasion was a multiethnic enterprise.[78] It is unclear, however, to what extent the word became widespread outside Athens. Herodotus tells us that the Spartans used the bland term *xeinoi* meaning "foreigners" to mean Persians. As Paul Cartledge has indicated to me in correspondence, the historian's point is that "the Spartans elided the key cultural distinction between Greek foreigners (*xeinoi*) and non-Greek foreigners (*barbaroi*) by calling all foreigners alike (*xeinoi*)."[79] We do not know what pejorative word, if any, the Persians used to describe the

Greeks. The Old Persian word *Yaunu*, which represented an attempt to reproduce the word "Ionian," was used to describe Greeks collectively, though we cannot rule out the possibility that this was in fact "a dismissive neutralization of the variety of Greek cultural and political experience."[80]

A strong indication that the Spartans judged themselves to be culturally superior to the Persians is evident in the speech that Herodotus puts into the mouth of the exiled Spartan king Demaratus, when Xerxes is reviewing his army and navy at the Hellespont. Asked by Xerxes whether the Spartans will have the courage to fight against the overwhelmingly superior Persian army, Demaratus replies, "Though free, they are not free in all aspects, for they have the law as their master, and they fear that much more than your men fear you."[81] Oriental characters appear in both tragedy and comedy, and are mocked.[82] In fifth-century art, the Persians become the quintessential barbarians, with the consequence that Amazons and Trojans are often depicted in Persian attire.[83]

It was the failure of the Persians to respect the holy places that perhaps chiefly led to the emergence of a racial stereotype, even though, as we have seen, they were merely paying the Athenians and Eretrians back in kind for destroying the temple in Sardis. It was a stereotype that was compounded of hierarchialism, effeminacy, and excessive luxuriousness. The fact is undeniable, however, that the Greco-Persian Wars also had a profound impact on Greek identity, both by sharpening the contrast between Greeks and non-Greeks and by bolstering the Greeks' sense of their cultural superiority, not least by their "invention of the barbarian," to use Edith Hall's evocative and influential phrase.[84] One consequence of this was that the Trojan War now took on the status of the original conflict between Persia and Greece—a status that was in part due to Xerxes' attempt to appropriate the poems of Homer for his own propagandistic purposes.[85]

We should not forget, as Geoffrey de Ste. Croix has pointed out, that "the magnificent achievements of the Greeks"—including the democratization of Athens and the victory over the Persians—"were partly due to the fact that their civilization was founded to a considerable degree on a slave basis," and we should not forget either that most ancient civilizations were founded to a considerable degree on a slave basis.[86]

Epilogue

THE BURNING OF ATHENS was a decisive moment in Athenian history. It both scarred the national psyche and helped shape it for the future, and the extraordinary cultural achievements of the next fifty years have to be weighed against the exploitation of fellow Greeks that resulted from the creation of the Delian Confederacy a year or so afterward. I confess I am profoundly moved by the extraordinary courage and self-sacrifice of the Athenians in the period from August 480 to June 479, when, forced out of their homeland, deprived of two harvests, and standing alone, they stalwartly refused all offers to make peace. Without their courage and self-sacrifice, we would not have the artistic, dramatic, philosophical, political, and scientific achievements that have illuminated Western civilization, though I resist the interpretation that it was the Battle of Salamis that "saved" the West. The West was still in danger, despite the spectacular victory. The Persians army was largely intact, Mardonius might have prevailed had he not sought a political solution, and the Battle of Plataea could have gone either way.

At the same time, it would be entirely wrong to stigmatize the Persian Empire as evil, any more than it would be accurate to stigmatize the Persians as effete, debauched, and barbaric. To their immense credit, their empire appears to have been remarkably inclusive. The king held absolute power, but his exercise of it was circumscribed by justice.[1] Indeed the behavior of the Athenians as an imperial power in the years that followed the Greek victory might well have seemed arrogant and high-handed to the Persians. For the slave population, including Sparta's helots, the salvation of Greece meant business as usual. For the Athenians, it meant that subjugation could take a new and uglier twist, cloaked in the rhetoric of political high-mindedness.

The year 480/79 also marks the traditional divide between the archaic and classical periods of Greek history. Though that is sometimes seen as a rather arbitrary division, there are good grounds for supposing that, when the Athenians returned to their homes and took the full measure of the destruction of their temples and tombs, they did indeed draw a line between the events of the past and what they imagined to lie ahead. No longer did the optimism that had been the hallmark of archaic sculpture seem appropriate. Life had become more serious and more precarious, and a more somber mood now prevailed.

From the Greek, especially Athenian, perspective, the Persian defeat was "formative and decisive."[2] It is debatable whether 480/79 was equally significant for the Persians. We've no credible evidence as to how many were slain on the Persian side. Of course, Persian propaganda would have minimized the scale of the defeats. Even if the losses were considerable, the population would have recovered easily within the space of a generation. The empire did not totter, and territorial setbacks were minimal. Even so, historians have sometimes argued that the rot had now set in and that the empire was on an irreversible decline. Perhaps. But it's by no means clear that defeat at the hands of the Greeks sent shock waves through the empire. It would, after all, last another 150 years, even though, as John Lee has aptly observed, Xerxes had "stirred up a hornet's nest," in consequence of which "every Persian king was going to have to deal with the aggressive, warlike Greeks buzzing around the western frontiers of the empire."[3]

The Achaemenid Empire was taken as a model by Reza Shah, a former brigadier general in the elite cavalry unit known as the Persian Cossack Brigade. In 1926 Reza Shah had himself crowned king of what became the Imperial State of Iran, Iran being the westernized form of the ancient name of Persia, Airyana Vaeja, which first occurs in the third century CE. Under his dynasty public buildings, including banks and post offices, were adorned with Achaemenid architectural motifs, just as banks and post offices in Greece have been adorned with classical and, in some cases, Mycenaean architectural motifs. Iranians seeking to connect themselves with their ancient heritage began naming their sons Daryush (Darius), Kambiz (Cambyses), and Kourosh (Cyrus). The name Xerxes

(Khshayarsha), however, never gained any popularity. In 1941 the invading British army forced Reza Shah to abdicate in favor of his son Mohammad Reza, who took the title Shahanshah, or "King of Kings." In 1971 he celebrated the two thousand five hundredth anniversary of the monarchy. "Sleep easily, Cyrus, for we are awake," he is said to have pronounced at Persepolis on this occasion.[4] The Pahlavi dynasty lasted until 1979, when it was overthrown in the Iranian Revolution. Mohammad Reza died in Egypt, where he had been granted asylum.

Athens burned many times subsequent to the Greco-Persian Wars. The next occasion after 479 was on the night of March 1, 86 BCE, when, following a five months' siege, the Roman general Sulla ordered his men to sack the city. A large

The Acropolis under Nazi occupation, April 1941. Courtesy of Bundesarchiv, Bild 101I-164-0389-23A/Scheerer/CC-BY-SA 3.0 (Wikimedia).

part of Athens went up in flames, though the city was spared the wholesale destruction that was meted out to the Piraeus at the same time.

In 267 CE the Herulians, a Gothic people who had swept into Greece from the Black Sea region, sacked Athens, despite the presence of a new city wall that the Roman emperor Valerian had recently provided. Many houses, as well as some public buildings, were burned.

In 395/6 Athens was sacked by Alaric the Goth, though the claim was later put about that the goddess Athena, martially attired, had appeared on the walls to repel the Gothic assault.

In the 470s the city was sacked by the Vandals and in 582 by the Slavs. On this latter occasion the burning was total. The city remained a ruin for two centuries.

On September 26, 1687, the Venetian commander Francesco Morosini set the Acropolis alight when he directed cannon fire against it from the nearby Hill of the Muses. The bombardment destroyed both the north and south walls of the Parthenon, which was serving as a gunpowder store and arsenal.

On October 26, 1821, during the Greek War of Independence, Greek freedom fighters attacked Athens and forced the Ottoman Turks to seek refuge on the Acropolis. Much damage was done to its buildings, since the Turks utilized the stones to build a makeshift fortification.

Finally, on April 27, 1941, the Nazis occupied Athens and erected a swastika over the Acropolis. Forty thousand inhabitants died of starvation. Athens, unburnt, was liberated on October 14, 1944.[5] This was followed by street fighting that culminated on December 3, when the occupying British forces supporting the royalist government opened fire on protesters who were demonstrating on behalf of the Communists.[6]

ACKNOWLEDGMENTS

I have benefited enormously from the erudition, attentiveness, and generosity of the two anonymous reviewers for Johns Hopkins University Press, as well as from the comments of my two dear friends, Paul Cartledge and Donald Lateiner, who read this book at various stages in its progress. For the maps I am indebted to the expertise of Michael Holobosky of Colgate University. I am most grateful to Tom Broughton-Willett for the immense care he took in preparing the index. I also wish to thank Niko Adamou, Tina Adamou, Anthony Aveni, Peter Balakian, Raffaella Dietz, Kiko Galvez, Graham Hodges, Carrie Keating, Steven Kepnes, Matt Leone, Jon Mikalson, John Naughton, Naomi Rood, Alan Swensen, and Robert Wilson for conversations, often compulsive and incisive, and unflagging support along life's road. All faults of fact and judgment are mine.

A NOTE ON SOURCES

Neither the Persians nor the Greeks kept official records of historical events, not that official records are intrinsically reliable. Or, if they did, none has survived. Neither side has bequeathed to us a single eyewitness account, unless we grant Aeschylus's *Persians* that status. People in antiquity didn't keep journals, and they didn't write memoirs when they retired. A serious limitation is that there are no Persian sources for the invasion, so our knowledge of it almost wholly reflects the perspective of the Greeks. That is one of the reasons why the names of the Persian kings are familiar to us only in their Greek form. It's worth bearing in mind that Darius was actually Darayavaush in Old Persian, while Xerxes was Khshayarsha. Adding to the difficulty of getting to the truth is the indisputable fact that Xerxes' invasion and the Greek response to it was pivotal in Western history. Hence, as Matt Waters observes, "Some hyperbole is inevitable for such a momentous historical event."[1]

What we have on the Persian side for the reign of Xerxes is thousands of clay tablets known collectively as the Fortification Archive and the Treasury Archive, mostly written in the Elamite language. These mainly describe the running of the Achaemenid Empire. We also have inscriptions, but though these tell us how Xerxes wanted to be perceived, they tell us little about his deeds. Largely their content is propaganda, such as summary references to conquests and building projects and lists of the subject peoples. Not surprisingly, given the monarchical structure of Persian society, they do not record any Persian defeat. We also have Babylonian and Egyptian documents that throw light on the effects of Persian imperialism outside the Persian homeland.[2]

Our only near-contemporary account of the invasion of Attica is provided by Aeschylus's *Persians*, which innovatingly presents Athens's naval victory at Salamis from the Persian perspective, albeit heavily colored with Athenian propaganda. Aeschylus fought at Marathon and probably at Salamis too. He puts sentiments into the mouths of his Persian characters that are flattering to the Greeks, and there are some lines that would have been greeted with cheers from his Athenian audience. Though a number of scholars claim that the play reflects the beginnings of the essentialist divide between Greeks and barbarians, it is not jingoistic.[3] And, as we have seen, the Messenger who brings news of the defeat says nothing of the destruction of the city.[4]

By far the most important source for the invasion is Herodotus, whom the Roman politician and orator Cicero dubbed the "father of history" but whom others have called "the father of lies." Herodotus, author of what we call the *Histories*, was a native of Halicarnassus in Caria, a city on the west coast of Turkey that had been under Persian domination for about three generations. Technically therefore he was born a Persian subject. Indeed, it is possible that he was driven into exile as a result of his opposition to the Persian-backed tyrant Lygdamis, the successor of Artemisia, the queen of Halicarnassus who fought at Salamis. Certainly Herodotus would have been very familiar with Persian culture, and he may even have had Persian acquaintances, if not friends.

It is important to note that there is nothing in his account of the Greco-Persian Wars to suggest that Herodotus believed the outcome owed anything to a cultural, far less to an ethnic divide, or even that the conflict represented a "clash of civilizations," to use an overworked phrase. Instead he presents the wars as a fight for freedom that the Greeks happened to win—rather fortuitously and despite their many deficiencies—against a very worthy adversary. Nor is the Persian army portrayed in an unflattering light. Herodotus reports that the reason why the Persians lost the Battle of Plataea was because "they were fighting unarmed against well-equipped hoplites."[5]

Herodotus has produced "a drama of religious and human significance which (moves) towards a predestined tragic end," as Nicholas Hammond writes.[6] He repeatedly depicts Xerxes as guilty of *hubris*—as "the archetype of an oriental despot practicing oriental boundlessness," one who failed to recognize divinely established boundaries. To counter this stereotype, recent studies, most notably that of Pierre Briant, have emphasized his solid accomplishments, including his vigorous architectural program at Persepolis and his consolidation of the legacy of his father Darius.[7]

Herodotus was only about five years old when Salamis was fought, so he was a generation younger than those with firsthand experience. He traveled widely—he was probably one of the most widely traveled men of his time. He visited Sardis and was familiar with part of the route that Xerxes took to Greece.[8] He read Aeschylus's *Persians*, to which his account is indebted, as, for instance, in his description of Xerxes viewing the battle seated on his throne in the foothills of Mount Aigaleos.[9]

The historian visited Athens, probably in the 440s, where he had the opportunity to interview veterans, many of them no doubt eager to recount their experiences. Most, however, were in their sixties by now, so their memories may have been somewhat defective, added to which they probably went in for a bit of embroidering. But that didn't mean their testimony was worthless. Oral history is an invaluable resource. Nor should we suppose that Herodotus was uncritical or that he believed everything his informants told him. Though he never credits any Athenian survivors with providing him with information, he does refer on two occasions to testimonies he heard secondhand,[10] and though he provides basic information about the evacuation of Attica, he largely limits himself to what was discussed and decided in the Assembly and Council.

To the detriment of this narrative, neither Herodotus nor any of his informants were interested in the logistics involved in evacuating by sea tens of thousands of people, after those same tens of thousands had carried out an internal evacuation by land, some having had to trek thirty miles or more on dirt tracks, persons of all ages, both in sickness and in health. Why did the double evacuation not strike him as comparable to many other "memorable deeds of the Greeks and the Persians" that he saw it as his mission to preserve, as he states at the beginning of his work? The answer, of course, is that humdrum details of this sort were of no particular interest to anyone in the ancient world, least of all to the elite reading public. Herodotus's silence is all the more striking from our twenty-first-century perspective in view of the length to which he goes to describe Xerxes' march. Here too, however, he has little to say about the logistics involved, though he was clearly fascinated by the bridging of the Hellespont and the cutting of the canal through Mount Athos.

Herodotus was intrigued by the Persians, and he gives considerable attention to their history, their institutions, and their national character. Indeed, as Donald Lateiner notes, "He admires the Persians more than any other foreign folk."[11] He seems, however, to have had limited familiarity with the Persian language.[12] Though we do not know how he acquired his data on them, as Rosaria Munson has pointed out, he would have had easy access to Persian informants.[13] These would have included the rank-and-file soldiers who served in the campaign, as well as members of the staff serving the satraps. Greeks who were employed in the Persian administration may also have provided him with privileged information. When at various times he writes "the Persians say," he is probably basing his opinion on a single source, and to what extent this single source represents a consensus viewpoint is unclear.[14] Though he cites the Persians as his source for the dream that Xerxes had circa 484 in which a tall, handsome man urges him to make preparations to invade Greece, it is possible that this anecdote was transmitted to him via Ionian informants. He does not claim to have used Persian sources for his narrative of the episodes covered by this book,[15] though he does cite the testimony of an unidentified Persian who predicted the defeat of the Persian army at Plataea.[16]

Herodotus's knowledge of the sack of the Acropolis may be based either on a Persian source or on the Peisistratid exiles who were in Xerxes' train, since he tells us that all the Athenian defenders were massacred. While purporting to record conversations that took place at the highest level, such as the conversation Xerxes has with his naval commanders just before the Battle of Salamis, he almost certainly fabricated them. He probably saw it as his business to explain to his readers the differences in opinion among the Persian high command in order to balance differences in opinion among the Greek high command, about which he did know something.[17] Ancient historians did not hold themselves to the same bar of accuracy as their modern counterparts try to do, particularly when it came to the spoken word.

In a rather unpleasant pamphlet called "On the Malice of Herodotus," the philosopher and biographer Plutarch, who lived five hundred years after Herodotus, accused him of being *philobarbaros*, a "barbarian lover." The allegation was not unconnected with the fact that Plutarch was a Boeotian, a member of one of the ethnic groups that medized. Though there is undoubted merit in the claim that Herodotus exhibits a striking lack of prejudice toward the Persians and other non-Greeks, this should not blind us to the fact that he reports as fact a number of instances of what Peter Green calls "atrocity propaganda"—acts of barbarism committed by the Persian king.[18] In other places either Herodotus or his source displays prejudices that call into question the accuracy of his account, notably with regard to Themistocles, whose reputation was besmirched by his political detractors after he was exiled at the end of the 470s.

The Athenian historian Thucydides (c. 460–400), who was a younger contemporary of Herodotus, discusses the Greco-Persian Wars briefly at the beginning of his *History of the Peloponnesian War*, as his work is usually called. However, what interests him most is not the wars themselves but Athens's decision to become a naval power. He hardly mentions the siege of Athens, and he adds little to Herodotus's account of the evacuation, though he does talk in some detail about the Themistoclean Wall, not least because he admired Themistocles greatly.

Ctesias of Cnidus, who was court physician to King Artaxerxes II of Persia from 405 to 398, wrote a work called *Persica* or *Persian Affairs* in twenty-three books, which purports to be a history of Persia from the rise of Assyria in the eighth century to the year 398 BCE.[19] All we have, however, are fragments, including an epitome written by Photius I, scholar and patriarch of Constantinople, in the ninth century CE. Unlike Herodotus, Ctesias offers a Persian perspective on the Greco-Persian Wars, though he entirely ignores the Ionian Revolt. Unlike Herodotus again, he gives the Spartans more credit for the victory than he does to the Athenians. (He also claims that "only two or three Spartans" perished at Thermopylae.) He or historians who quote him occasionally commit blunders, most egregiously by placing the Battle of Plataea before the Battle of Salamis.

Diodorus Siculus, living in the middle of the first century BCE, wrote a universal history, book 11, chapters 1–37 of which cursorily describes the Greco-Persian Wars. Scholars believe that his account of the Battle of Salamis was based on the no-longer extant work of a fourth-century BCE historian called Ephorus of Cyme. Diodorus claims that he read Ctesias of Cnidus, but there is no evidence that he made use of his account of Xerxes' invasion, which is probably just as well.[20]

Plutarch (c. 45–120), who lived in the Roman Empire, wrote a life both of Themistocles, the most important Athenian in our story, and of his contemporaries Aristides and Cimon. He provides a brief but detailed picture of the evacuation, though we cannot be sure how accurate his account is, since he is writing so long after the event and may be reliant on oral history. Some at least of what he writes may fall into the category of "what must have happened" when the Athenians evacuated.

Lastly, the travel writer Pausanias, who flourished in the middle of the second century CE, wrote a *Description of Greece* that includes some details relating to the sack of the Acropolis, most notably those which have to do with the monuments that the Persians filched or destroyed.

In addition to the literary evidence, we have archaeology. Archaeology provides us with a compelling picture of the violent destruction of the temples and statues on the Acropolis, notably of the Older Parthenon and of the statues that were buried after the Persian sack, of civic buildings in the Agora, and of the temples at Rhamnous and

Sunium. It also testifies to the pollution of wells and to the haste with which the Them-istoclean Wall was constructed. What archaeology fails to indicate, however, is the scale of the devastation in both the Attic countryside and the residential area of the city. Athenian houses were made largely of mudbrick and these, when destroyed, leave little trace in the archaeological record. Perhaps most frustrating of all, there is no evi-dence for the circuit wall that preceded the Themistoclean Wall. Other useful sources include inscriptions and art.

To conclude, much that relates to the Persian invasion of Attica is obscure, though this has not deterred modern historians from writing confident accounts of what "actu-ally happened." I have tried my best to be insightful, but I have kept my imagination on a tight rein. For this reason, I have flagged (tediously, I suspect) my uncertainties with adverbs like "possibly," "probably," and the like. Even so, much of what I have written is in places necessarily speculative.

All history is a dialogue between the present and the past across an invisible vacuum filled with unrecoverable detail.

NOTES

PROLOGUE

1. Thucydides 1.90.3.

CHAPTER 1. THE ORIGINS

1. M. T. Waters, *Ancient Persia: A Concise History of the Achaemenid Empire, 550–330 BCE* (Cambridge: Cambridge University Press 2014) 122.

2. J. Wiesehöfer, "The Achaemenid Empire," in I. Morris and W. Scheidel (eds.), *Dynamics of Ancient Empires: State Power from Assyria to Byzantium* (Oxford: Oxford University Press 2009) 77.

3. Aeschylus, *Persians* 584–90.

4. J. Haubold, "Xerxes' Homer," in E. Bridges, E. Hall, and P. J. Rhodes (eds.), *Cultural Responses to the Persian Wars: Antiquity to the Third Millennium* (Oxford: Oxford University Press 2007) 49.

5. J. Boardman, *The Greeks in Asia* (London: Thames and Hudson 2015) 29.

6. R. V. Munson, in R. V. Munson (ed.), *Oxford Readings in Classical Studies: Herodotus*, vol. 2 (Oxford: Oxford University Press 2013) 334.

7. Herodotus 7.13.3.

8. Herodotus 9.16.5.

9. Herodotus 7.19.1.

10. Herodotus 3.134.5.

11. For Achaemenid religion, see W. Henkelman, *The Other Gods Who Are: Studies in Elamite-Iranian Acculturation Based on the Persepolis Fortification Texts*, Achaemenid History 14 (Leiden: Nederlands Instituut voor het Nabije Oosten 2008).

12. The Cyrus Cylinder, sometimes misleadingly described as "the first charter of human rights," refers to the return of the people whose dwellings had been ruined during Babylonian rule when Cyrus captured Babylon in 539. For the text, see A. Kuhrt, *The Persian Empire: A Corpus of Sources* (London: Routledge 2009), 1:70–74, ll. 30–32.

13. M. H. Hansen and T. H. Nielsen (eds.), *An Inventory of Archaic and Classical Poleis* (Oxford: Oxford University Press 2004) 53.

14. S. Hornblower, *The Greek World, 479–323 BC* (London: Methuen 1983) 14.

15. Herodotus 8.30.

16. Herodotus 5.97.2.

17. A. Kuhrt, *The Ancient Near East, c. 3000–330 BC* (London: Routledge 1995) 693–94.

18. Plutarch, *Themistocles* 1.1.

19. R. Thomas, *Literacy and Orality in Ancient Greece* (Cambridge: Cambridge University Press 1992), points out that classical Greece was very much an oral society, one in which the written word was secondary to the spoken. Many regions of the Persian world were also literate, including Egypt, Ionia, Mesopotamia, and Phoenicia.

20. D. M. Lewis, "Persians in Herodotus," in M. H. Jameson (ed.), *The Greek Historians: Literature and History; Papers Presented to A. E. Raubitschek* (Saratoga, CA: Anma Libri 1985) 104.

21. N. F. Jones, *Politics and Society in Ancient Greece* (Westport, CT: Praeger 2008) 41–42.

22. Critias, DK 88 B37 (H. A. Diels, *Fragmente der Vorsokratiker*, 6th ed., rev. by W. Kranz [Berlin: Wiedmann 1952]).

23. Herodotus 1.153.1.

24. Herodotus 5.73.2.

25. P. Georges, "Persian Ionia under Darius: The Revolt Reconsidered," *Historia* 49.1 (2000) 1–39, notes that Darius's conquest of Scythia and the Thracian hinterland greatly benefited the East Greeks by providing them with a source of silver for the minting of coins.

26. Herodotus 5.97.2.

27. Herodotus 5.96.2.

28. Herodotus 5.103.1.

29. Herodotus 5.102.1.

30. Herodotus 6.21.2.

31. Herodotus 5.105.2.

32. Herodotus 6.101.2–3. For the destruction of Eretria, see J. M. Hall, *Artifact and Artifice: Classical Archaeology and the Ancient Historian* (Chicago: University of Chicago Press 2014) 35–54.

33. See R. S. J. Garland, *Wandering Greeks: From the Time of Homer to the Death of Alexander the Great* (Princeton: Princeton University Press 2014) appendix E ("Catalogue of the Enslaved") 271–77, for a list of Greeks who were enslaved by non-Greeks, Greeks who enslaved non-Greeks, and Greeks who enslaved other Greeks.

34. Herodotus 8.1.2, 8.46.2, and 9.28.5.

35. Hall, *Artifact and Artifice*, 38, citing P. Auberson, *Eretria*, vol. 1: *Temple d'Apollon Daphnéphoros; Architecture* (Berne: Editions Francke 1968) 10.

36. Herodotus does not provide us with any figures of the sizes of the two armies. For further discussion, see P. Krentz, *The Battle of Marathon* (New Haven: Yale University Press 2010) 91–92, 102.

37. See J. W. I. Lee, "Hoplite Warfare in Herodotus," appendix N, in R. B. Strassler (ed.), *The Landmark Herodotus: The Histories* (New York: Pantheon Books 2007) 798–804. For estimates of the weight of hoplite armor, see Krentz, *The Battle of Marathon*, 50.

38. For the number of the Persian dead, see J. Hyland, "Contesting Marathon: Billows, Krentz, and the Persian Problem," *Classical Philology* 106.3 (2011) 274–75. Herodotus does not reveal his source, nor can we conclude that a precise count of the enemy dead would have been conducted.

39. It was supposedly at this spot in 1809 that Lord Byron "dreamed that Greece might still be free."

40. A. P. Matthaiou in P. Derow and R. Parker (eds.), *Herodotus and His World: Essays from a Conference in Honor of George Forrest* (Oxford: Oxford University Press 2003) 199–200, gives details of the monument in Athens to the Marathonian dead.

41. Pausanias 1.32.5. See J. M. Camp, *The Archaeology of Athens* (New Haven: Yale University Press 2001) 47.

42. Pausanias 1.32.3.

43. Herodotus 7.1.1.

44. See A. Kuhrt, *The Persian Empire* vol. 1 (London: Routledge 2007) no. 88 (p. 304).

45. Herodotus 7.5–9.

46. Aeschylus, *Persians* 754–59.

47. J. F. Lazenby, *The Defence of Greece, 490–479 BC* (Warminster: Aris and Philips 1993) 205, writes, "[T]o the Persians [Greece] could only ever have been a relatively unimportant and, no doubt, troublesome province on the empire's fringes," but I believe this underestimates the seriousness of Xerxes' commitment to conquest.

48. H. D. Wallinga, *Xerxes' Greek Adventure: The Naval Perspective* (Leiden: Brill 2005) 30.

49. R. Osborne, *Greek History* (London: Routledge 2004) 80.

50. Herodotus 7.20.1. For the date of the Babylonian revolt, see C. Waarzeggers, "The Babylonian Revolts against Xerxes and the 'End of Archives,'" *Archiv für Orientforschung* 50 (2003–4) 150–73; and A. Kuhrt, "Reassessing the Reign of Xerxes in the Light of New Evidence," in M. Kozuh et al. (eds.), *Extraction and Control: Studies in Honor of Matthew W. Stolper*, Studies in Ancient Oriental Civilization 68 (Chicago: Oriental Institute of the University of Chicago 2014) 163–69.

51. Herodotus 7.8.γ 1–2. See D. Lateiner, *The Historical Method of Herodotus* (Toronto: University of Toronto Press 1989) 129.

52. Aeschylus, *Persians* 74, memorably describes it as "the herd of populous Asia."

53. M. Flower, "The Size of Xerxes' Expeditionary Force," appendix R, in R. B. Strassler (ed.), *The Landmark Herodotus: The Histories* (New York: Pantheon Books 2007) 822, favors the lower limit of forty to fifty thousand infantry.

54. Herodotus 7.25.2.

55. Herodotus 7.19.2.

56. Herodotus 7.61–88.

57. Flower, "The Size of Xerxes' Expeditionary Force," 822.

58. Herodotus 7.89.1. Wallinga, *Xerxes' Greek Adventure*, 42–43. Flower, "The Size of Xerxes' Expeditionary Force," 823.

59. Herodotus 7.38–39.

60. R. Rollinger, "Herodotus and the Intellectual Heritage of the Ancient Near East," in S. Aro and R. M. Whiting (eds.), *The Heirs of Assyria: Proceedings of the Opening Symposium of the Assyrian and Babylonian Intellectual Heritage Project Held in Tvarminne, Finland, October 8–11, 1998*, Melammu Symposia 1 (Helsinki: Eisenbrauns 2000) esp. 66–70, points out striking parallels between Herodotus's account and a purificatory ritual performed by the Hittites after a military defeat. A similar story is told of Xerxes' predecessor Darius slaughtering three sons whose father had requested that they be released from military service at the start of his Scythian campaign (Herodotus 4.84).

61. See A. Kuhrt, *The Persian Empire: A Corpus of Sources from the Achaemenid Period*, vol. 2 (London: Routledge 2007) no. 695 (p. 722), where a Babylonian cavalry officer agrees to perform military service on behalf of another, on condition that the latter provides him with a suit of armor and five hundred grams of silver.

62. Plutarch, *Themistocles* 19.4.

63. Plutarch, *Themistocles* 22.1–2, reports seeing a small statue of Themistocles in the Temple of Artemis Aristoboule in Athens.

64. J. S. Morrison, J. F. Coates, and N. B. Rankov, *The Athenian Trireme*, rev. ed. (Cambridge: Cambridge University Press 2000) 250 and 252, cited in R. Lane Fox, *The Classical World: An Epic History from Homer to Hadrian* (New York: Basic Books 2014) 98.

65. For the development of the Athenian fleet, see R. S. J. Garland, *The Piraeus: From the Fifth to the First Century BC*, 2nd ed. (London: Gerald Duckworth 2001) 14–19. For the scale of shipbuilding activity, see Peter Green, *The Greco-Persian Wars* (Berkeley: University of California 1996) 57.

66. Herodotus 7.36. See also Aeschylus, *Persians* 68–73. The Greek historian Arrian was skeptical as to whether the Hellespont could be bridged by warships (*Anabasis* 5.7.2), while the Roman poet Juvenal deemed the story to be one "that the lying Greeks dare to claim to be historical" (*Satires* 10.174–6). N. G. L. Hammond and L. J. Roseman, "The Construction of Xerxes' Bridge over the Hellespont," *Journal of Hellenic Studies* 116 (1996) 88–107, deduce that the bridges were "well within the capability of the engineers of the day to design and build" (p. 95) and that "most of the ships are likely to have been penteconters" (p. 98).

67. Herodotus 7.22.1. See N. G. L. Hammond, "The Expedition of Xerxes," in John Boardman, N. G. L. Hammond, D. M. Lewis, and M. Ostwald (eds.), *Cambridge Ancient History*, 2nd ed., vol. 4: *Persia, Greece and the Western Mediterranean, c.525 to 479 BC* (Cambridge: Cambridge University Press 1988) 526.

68. The fact that the Persians, like the Greeks, venerated flowing water further renders the charge of whipping the Hellespont suspect (Herodotus 1.138).

69. Herodotus 7.34–35.

70. In a talk given at the annual meeting of the Society for the Promotion of Hellenic Studies, London, June 14, 2014, Christopher Carey, "On the Road with Xerxes," suggested that a pontoon bridge might not last even a year, given the combined conditions of wind and currents.

71. Herodotus 7.26.3. The town of Kelainai is probably as far east as Herodotus reached in the course of his travels.

72. Herodotus 7.40.2–41. "Fancy" is my translation of *logos*. A more literal translation would be "whenever the reason seized him."

73. P. Briant, *From Cyrus to Alexander: A History of the Persian Empire*, trans. P. T. Daniels (Winona Lake, IN: Eisenbrauns 2002) 526.

74. Aeschylus, *Persians* 753–58.

75. Herodotus 7.132.1. "Medize" derives from the Greek verb *mēdizō*, meaning to "side with the Medes." The Medes were northern neighbors of the Persians. They were prominent from the eighth to the sixth century. See A. Kuhrt, *The Ancient Near East, c. 3000–330* (London: Routledge 1995) 2:652–56. One possible reason why the Greeks talked of medizing rather than "persianizing" is because the Medes came first in the phrase. Another, as Paul Cartledge has suggested to me, is that the use of the verb *mēdizō* was intentionally belittling of the Persians.

76. Herodotus 7.43.1. See P. Georges, *Barbarian Asia and the Greek Experience: From the Archaic Period to the Age of Xenophon* (Baltimore: Johns Hopkins University Press 1994) 60; J. Haubold, "Xerxes' Homer," in E. Bridges, E. Hall, and P. J. Rhodes (eds.), *Cultural Responses to the Persian Wars: Antiquity to the Third Millennium* (Oxford: Oxford University Press 2007) 55.

77. Haubold, "Xerxes' Homer," 54–58.

78. Herodotus 7.33, 9.116; cf. Homer, *Iliad* 2.701–2. See D. Boedeker, "Protesilaos and the End of Herodotus' *Histories*," *Classical Antiquity* 7 (1988) 30–48.

79. Herodotus 7.56.1.

80. Herodotus 7.115.3.

81. Herodotus 7.116.

82. P. A. Cartledge, *After Thermopylae: The Oath of Plataea and the End of the Graeco-Persian Wars* (Oxford: Oxford University Press 2013) 62.

83. Herodotus 7.145.1.

84. Hammond, "The Expedition of Xerxes," 543–45.

85. Herodotus 8.3.1.

86. The so-called Serpent Column, a dedication made after the war at Delphi, records the names of cities that joined the alliance, though it "only goes to reinforce the politics of the war," as Robin Osborne, *Greece in the Making, 1200–479 BC* (London: Routledge 1996; 2nd ed. 2009) 341, notes, since some of the cities that participated are not included. See R. Meiggs and D. Lewis (eds.), *A Selection of Greek Historical Inscriptions to the End of the Fifth Century BC*, rev. ed. (Oxford: Clarendon Press 1988) 27 = C. W. Fornara, *Archaic Times to the End of the Peloponnesian War*, 2nd ed. (Cambridge: Cambridge University Press 1983) 59.

87. Herodotus 7.175.1.

CHAPTER 2. THE EVACUATION

1. Cited in Plutarch, *Moral Precepts* 404d–e = H. A. Diels, *Fragmente der Vorsokratiker*, 6th ed., rev. by W. Kranz (Berlin: Wiedmann 1952) 1:86.

2. Herodotus 7.140–42.

3. T. Holland, *Persian Fire* (New York: Little, Brown 2005) 250.

4. M. Scott, *Delphi: A History of the Center of the Ancient World* (Princeton: Princeton University Press 2014) 9–30, provides an account of the procedure for consulting the Delphic Oracle based on the latest archaeological findings. See also J. Hall, "Delphic Vapours," in *Artifact and Artifice: Classical Archaeology and the Ancient Historian* (Chicago: University of Chicago Press 2014) 17–34.

5. Sophocles, *Oedipus the King* ll. 787–93.

6. Herodotus 7.140.2.

7. Herodotus 6.19.2.

8. N. G. L. Hammond, "The Expedition of Xerxes," in John Boardman, N. G. L. Hammond, D. M. Lewis, and M. Ostwald (eds.), *Cambridge Ancient History*, 2nd ed., vol. 4: *Persia, Greece and the Western Mediterranean, c.525 to 479 BC* (Cambridge: Cambridge University Press 1988) 540.

9. Herodotus 7.141.2.

10. Herodotus 7.141.3–4.

11. J. Fontenrose, *The Delphic Oracle: Its Responses and Operations* (Berkeley: University of California Press 1978), who has examined all the forty-nine oracles cited by Herodotus, concludes that not a single one is authentic. As Jon Mikalson, *Herodotus and Religion in the Persian Wars* (Chapel Hill: University of North Carolina Press 2003) 56, points out, "Missing in Herodotus are the machinations of the priests, the workshop of the poets, and the chasms, caves, vapors, and psychedelic mushrooms that late sources and modern scholars attempt to attribute to the Delphi oracle."

12. Herodotus 7.142–43. For Themistocles' inspired interpretation, see R. S. J. Garland, *Introducing New Gods: The Politics of Athenian Religion*, 2nd ed. (Ithaca: Cornell University Press 1992) 64–68.

13. R. A. Tomlinson, *Greek Sanctuaries* (New York: St. Martin's Press 1976) 82.

14. Herodotus 7.142.2.

15. Herodotus 7.143.3.

16. The earliest reference to the belief that the Athenians were autochthonous occurs in Pindar's *Second Isthmian Ode* (l. 19), dated 470 BCE.

17. Herodotus 7.139.2.

18. Diodorus Siculus 11.14.5.

19. For the text of the decree, see R. Meiggs and D. Lewis (eds.), *A Selection of Greek Historical Inscriptions to the End of the Fifth Century BC*, rev. ed. (Oxford: Clarendon Press 1988) no. 23. For translation and commentary, see C. W. Fornara, *Archaic Times to the End of the Peloponnesian War*, 2nd ed. (Cambridge: Cambridge University Press 1983) no. 55. M. H. Jameson, "Waiting for the Barbarian: New Light on the Persian Wars," *Greece & Rome*, 2nd ser., 8 (1961) 5–18, dated the decree to the end of 481. N. G. L. Hammond, "The Narrative of Herodotus VII and the Decree of Themistocles at Troezen," *Journal of Hellenic Studies* 102 (1982) 75–93, is useful on matters of chronology. See also H. Bowden, *Classical Athens and the Delphic Oracle: Divination and Democracy* (Cambridge: Cambridge University Press 2005) 100–107.

20. G. Cawkwell, *The Greek Wars: The Failure of Persia* (Oxford: Oxford University Press 2005) appendix 6 (pp. 277–80). Similarly, J. F. Lazenby, *The Defence of Greece, 490–479 BC* (Warminster: Aris & Phillips 1993) 104, describes the decree as "more than likely . . . basically a patriotic fabrication of the fourth century, put in its final form in the third."

21. A. R. Burn, *Persia and the Greeks: The Defense of the West, 546–478*, 2nd ed. (Stanford, CA: Stanford University Press 1984) 360.

22. Meiggs and Lewis, *A Selection of Greek Historical Inscriptions to the End of the Fifth Century BC*, 50.

23. Herodotus 8.60 β. There is confusion among the sources. Both Cicero, *On Duties* 3.48, and Cornelius Nepos, *Life of Themistocles* 2.8.1, mention only Salamis and Troezen as destinations. Aelius Aristides 46.192 claims that the women and children went to Troezen, whereas the elderly went to Salamis.

24. Herodotus 6.89.

25. Thucydides 1.93.4; cf. Herodotus 7.144.1.

26. B. Strauss, *The Battle of Salamis* (New York: Simon and Schuster 2004) 60.

27. Herodotus 6.49–50, 73.

28. S. M. Burstein, "The Themistocles Decree," *California Studies in Classical Antiquity* 4 (1971) 103, argues that the wording of the decree, specifically the phrase "depart for Salamis," suggests that the exiles "have already returned to Athens but that no decision has yet been made about their future."

29. Burstein, "The Themistocles Decree," 107–8.

30. Mikalson, *Herodotus and Religion in the Persian Wars*, 59.

31. D. Whitehead, *The Demes of Attica, 508/7–ca. 250 BC: A Political and Social Study* (Princeton: Princeton University Press 1986) 122.

32. See R. S. J. Garland, *Wandering Greeks: The Ancient Greek Diaspora from the Time of Homer to the Death of Alexander the Great* (Princeton: Princeton University Press 2014) 99–113.

33. Thucydides 2.14.

34. Herodotus 8.68 β 2. The probability that Herodotus thought Artemisia to be correct in her view is strengthened by the fact that he elsewhere shows respect toward her judgment, perhaps in part because she was a compatriot of Halicarnassus (8.87–88, 8.101–3).

35. Homer, *Iliad* 2.762; Herodotus 6.95.1.

36. Plutarch, *Themistocles* 10.5.

37. Plutarch, *Themistocles* 10.6.

38. R. S. J. Garland, *The Greek Way of Death*, 2nd ed. (London: Bristol Classical Press, 2001) 104–20.

39. M. C. Taylor, *Salamis and the Salaminioi: The History of an Unofficial Athenian Demos* (Amsterdam: J. C. Gieben 1997) 21. Her conclusion is based on her interpretation of *Inscriptiones Graecae* (*IG*) I³ 1, a fragmentary Athenian decree that grants the right to reside on Salamis subject to certain conditions. The sea level has risen some five feet since antiquity. See N. G. L. Hammond, "Salamis, Attica," in R. Stillwell (ed.), *The Princeton Encyclopedia of Classical Sites* (Princeton: Princeton University Press 1976) 796–97.

40. Taylor, *Salamis and the Salaminioi*, 127.

41. These and similar issues relating to modern-day refugee settlement are discussed in *Refugee Health: An Approach to Emergency Situations* (Médecins Sans Frontières) in http://refbooks.msf.org/msf_docs/en/refugee_health/rh.pdf.

42. Plutarch, *Themistocles* 10.3.

43. The topography of Thermopylae has changed a great deal since antiquity. The calcites from the hot springs have created a much more even descent where the pass once was, the cliffs have fallen into the sea, and the sea has retreated over half a mile from the original coastline, mainly due to alluvial deposit from the River Spercheios. See K. Vouvalidis, "Palaeogeographical Reconstruction of the Battle Terrain in Ancient Thermopylae, Greece," *Geodinamica Acta* 12 (2010) 241–53. For the battle itself, see P. A. Cartledge, *Thermopylae: The Battle That Changed the World* (Woodstock: Overlook Press, 2006).

44. Pausanias 3.4.8.

45. Herodotus 7.220.2.

46. Herodotus 8.24.

47. Herodotus 7.228.2.

48. Pausanias 3.14.

49. Herodotus 8.18.

50. P. Green, *The Greco-Persian War* (Berkeley: University of California Press 1996) 153.

51. Herodotus 8.25.2.

52. Herodotus 8.27.5. R. C. S. Felsch (ed.), *Kalapodi II. Ergebnisse der Ausgrabungen im Heligtum der Artemis und des Apollon von Hyampolis in der antiken Phokis* (Mainz am Rhein: Phillip von Zabern 2007) 16, provides archaeological evidence for the violent destruction of the sanctuary.

53. See Herodotus 8.33; cf. 35, 50.2.

54. Herodotus 8.37–39.

55. Lazenby, *The Defence of Greece, 490–479 BC*, 151.

56. Herodotus 8.41.1. The fact that only a proclamation (*kērugma*) was issued at this point lends further support to the theory that there were two evacuations, one orderly, the other emergency, the original *psēphisma* or decree being already in effect.

57. Herodotus 8.71.2.

58. Plutarch, *Themistocles* 9.4.

59. Plutarch, *Themistocles* 10.1.

60. Plutarch, *Cimon* 5.3.

61. [Aristotle], *Constitution of Athens* 23.1.

62. Herodotus 8.40.1.

CHAPTER 3. THE FIRST BURNING

1. Aeschylus, *Persians* 809–12.

2. Herodotus 7.41.1.

3. H. T. Wallinga, *Xerxes' Greek Adventure* (Leiden: Brill 2005) 22–31, believes that it was Athens's naval buildup that prompted Xerxes to undertake the expedition.

4. Pausanias 3.16.7–8.

5. J. M. Camp, *The Archaeology of Athens* (New Haven: Yale University Press 2001) 126.

6. J. Travlos, *Pictorial Dictionary of Ancient Athens* (London: Thames and Hudson 1971) 158, notes that no trace of the archaic city wall has come to light and "the line it took is a matter of informed conjecture."

7. Herodotus 5.71 and Thucydides 1.126.

8. Herodotus 5.64–65.

9. Herodotus 5.72.

10. Herodotus 8.51.2.

11. [Aristotle], *Constitution of Athens* 23.1.

12. Plutarch, *Themistocles* 10.4.

13. Herodotus 8.52.2.

14. Herodotus 9.49.2. He claims that the Scythians used the same tactic against the Persians (4.120 and 140).

15. K. Lynch, *The Symposium in Context: Pottery from a Late Archaic House near the Athenian Agora, Hesperia* suppl. 46 (Princeton: American School of Classical Studies at Athens 2011) 27.

16. Herodotus 8.52.1. N. G. L. Hammond, "The Expedition of Xerxes," in John Boardman, N. G. L. Hammond, D. M. Lewis, and M. Ostwald (eds.), *Cambridge Ancient History*, 2nd ed., vol. 4: *Persia, Greece and the Western Mediterranean, c.525 to 479 BC* (Cambridge: Cambridge University Press 1988) 565, states that some of the Persian arrowheads came to light in excavations, but I have not found any other report of this.

17. Herodotus 8.52.2.

18. Herodotus 8.53.1.

19. J. F. Hurwit, *The Athenian Acropolis: History, Mythology, and Archaeology from the Neolithic Era to the Present* (Cambridge: Cambridge University Press 1999) 136.

20. Hammond, "The Expedition of Xerxes," 565. A similar story was reported in the *Daily Mail*, June 9, 1941, of a Greek soldier called Konstantinos Koukidis who threw himself off the Acropolis—wrapped in a Greek flag—rather than surrender to the Nazis. A plaque on the flank of the Acropolis celebrates his deed, even though the Greek Army Historical Department concluded in April 2000 that there was no evidence of either Koukidis or his deed. See http://www.drgeorgepc.com/NightAcropolis.pdf. I.

21. Ctesias of Cnidus (Felix Jacoby [ed.], *Die Fragmente der griechischen Historiker* [*FGrH*] 688 F 13) claims that some of the defenders escaped in the night before the Persians captured the Acropolis.

22. Pausanias 1.26.6.

23. Pausanias 1.27.1.

24. As to whether "Hundred-footer" is another name for the Older Parthenon or the descriptive title of a (hypothetical) predecessor to the Older Parthenon, see R. A. Tomlinson, *Greek Sanctuaries* (New York: St. Martin's Press 1976) 81.

25. Travlos, *Pictorial Dictionary of Ancient Athens*, pl. 567, shows the poros foundations of the Older Parthenon with workers standing on the bedrock.

26. See D. Müller, *Topographischer Bildkommentar zu den Historien Herodot: Griechenland* (Tübingen: Ernst Wasmuth 1987) pl. 8 (p. 614) for a picture of the remains of the southwest corner of the Old Propylon.

27. For the Acropolis before the Persian destruction, see H. R. Goette, *Athens, Attica, and the Megarid: An Archaeological Guide* (London: Routledge 1993) 5–11.

28. For the freestanding archaic sculpture on the Acropolis knocked down by the Persians, see H. Payne and G. M. Young, *Archaic Marble Sculpture from the Acropolis*, 2nd ed. (London: Cresset Press 1950).

29. Hurwit, *The Athenian Acropolis*, 136.

30. T. Holland, *Persian Fire: The First World Empire and the Battle for the West* (New York: Little, Brown 2005) 305.

31. Plato, *Laws* 7.796b.

32. For the destruction of the Agora, see J. M. Camp, *The Athenian Agora: Excavations in the Heart of Classical Athens*, rev. ed. (London: Thames and Hudson 1992) 35–38 and 59–60.

33. Arrian, *Anabasis* 3.16.7–8.

34. Thucydides 6.53–59. See E. A. Meyor, "Thucydides on Harmodius and Aristogeiton, Tyranny and History," *Classical Quarterly* 58.1 (May 2008) 13–34.

35. Plutarch, *Themistocles* 31.1.

36. Herodotus 8.71.1.

37. Herodotus 8.99.1. The anecdote may well be an invention, intended to draw further attention to Xerxes' *hubris*.

38. Herodotus 5.71.

39. Herodotus 8.55.

40. J. D. Mikalson, *Herodotus and Religion in the Persian Wars* (Chapel Hill: University of North Carolina Press 2003) 73.

41. Pausanias 1.27.2.

42. Diodorus Siculus 11.14.5 and 16.2.

43. See R. Parker, *Miasma* (Oxford: Clarendon Press 1983) 276. The inference is from Herodotus 7.133.2.

44. Herodotus 9.7 β. See T. E. Gregory, *Isthmia V: The Hexamilion and the Fortress* (Princeton: American School of Classical Studies at Athens 1993) 5 and 25–26.

45. Aeschylus, *Persians* 339–40.

46. Herodotus 8.56. See also Diodorus Siculus 11.16.1, who claims that near panic broke out among the sailors when they saw the size of the Persian fleet.

47. Plutarch, *Themistocles* 2.4. Plutarch in his essay entitled "On the Malice of Herodotus" alleged that the anecdote about Mnesiphilus was invented by Herodotus to discredit Themistocles for falsely claiming to be the originator of the plan to fight at Salamis (*Moralia* 869d–f). See F. J. Frost, "Themistocles and Mnesiphilus," *Historia* 20.1 (1971) 20–25.

48. Herodotus 8.68.

49. Herodotus 8.58.2.

50. Herodotus 8.61. See too Plutarch, *Themistocles* 11.2–5, who has the exchange take place between Themistocles and Eurybiades. To the taunt that the Athenians had abandoned their homes and walls, Themistocles replies, "We did not think it fitting to be slaves to inanimate objects."

51. Herodotus 8.62.2.

52. J. F. Lazenby, *The Defence of Greece, 490–479 BC* (Warminster: Aris and Phillips 1993) 158.

53. Herodotus 7.143.3.

54. M. H. Hansen, and T. H. Nielsen (eds.), *An Inventory of Archaic and Classical Poleis* (Oxford: Oxford University Press 2004) 294 col 1.

55. See R. S. J. Garland, *Wandering Greeks: The Ancient Greek Diaspora from the Age of Homer to the Death of Alexander the Great* (Princeton: Princeton University Press 2014), 57–78.

56. Thucydides 7.77.7. I am grateful to Paul Cartledge for pointing me to this passage.

57. Herodotus 3.147, 6.18–20.

58. Herodotus 8.70.2.

59. Herodotus 8.75–76. See also Aeschylus, *Persians* 353–60. Aeschylus, who does not name Sicinnus, describes him as "an avenger or malignant spirit."

60. C. Hignett, *Xerxes' Invasion of Greece* (Oxford: Clarendon Press 1963) 407.

61. Herodotus 8.75.2.

62. When Themistocles was ostracized from Athens in the 460s, he wrote to Xerxes' son Artaxerxes I claiming that he was an exile "because of my friendship for you" (Thucydides 1.137.4).

63. Herodotus 8.75.1.

64. Aeschylus, *Persians* 369–71.

65. P. Green, *Xerxes at Salamis* (New York: Praeger 1970), 186.

66. Herodotus 8.86.

67. Diodorus Siculus 11.18–19.

68. Herodotus 8.78. We should hardly suppose that Aristides returned from exile on the eve of the battle. He and Xanthippus had evidently been elected general in 480/79, which means that they must have returned to Athens in 481/0. It is unclear why Aristides was in Aegina just before the battle.

69. Herodotus 8.83.

70. Plutarch, *Themistocles* 14.2.

71. Aeschylus, *Persians* 428.

72. Both Aeschylus (*Persians* 336–43) and Herodotus (7.89) claim the Persian fleet comprised 1,207 ships, though M. Flower, "The Size of Xerxes' Expeditionary Force," appendix R in R. B. Strassler, *The Landmark Herodotus: The Histories* (New York: Pantheon Books 2007) 823, suggests it comprised between 300 to 400 ships, which would have made it about equal in size to the Greek fleet.

73. Diodorus Siculus 11.19.3. See A. R. Burn, *Persia and the Greeks* (Stanford: Stanford University Press 1984) 467.

74. Psyttalia has been identified both with Haghios Georghios in the middle of the channel and with Lipsokoutali outside the channel. See N. G. L. Hammond, "Salamis,

Attica," in R. Stillwell (ed.), *The Princeton Encyclopedia of Classical Sites* (Princeton: Princeton University Press 1976) 796–97.

75. Aeschylus, *Persians* 447–64.

76. Herodotus 8.96.1.

77. Aeschylus, *Persians* 465.

78. Tearing one's clothes was a public display of grief in the ancient world, well documented in the Hebrew Bible, the first mention being in Genesis 37:29 and 34 in relation to the Joseph story.

79. Herodotus 8.90.3; cf. Diodorus Siculus 11.19.4.

80. Herodotus 8.98.1. This sentence is inscribed on the General Post Office in New York City at 8th Avenue. The translation is by George H. Palmer.

81. Aeschylus, *Persians* 424.

82. Herodotus 8.99.2.

83. B. Strauss, *Salamis: The Naval Encounter That Saved Greece—and Western Civilization* (New York: Simon and Schuster 2004) 211–12.

84. Herodotus 8.89.

85. See further C. N. Rados, *La Bataille de Salamine* (Paris: Fontemoing & Cie 1915) 365–66.

86. For the location of the mole, see Hammond, "The Expedition of Xerxes," 569–70.

87. Both Ctesias (*FGrH* 688 F 13.26) and Aristodemus (*FGrH* 104 F1) suggest that Xerxes began building a causeway between Phaleron and Salamis before the battle. For arguments against, see Lazenby, *The Defence of Greece, 490–79 BC*, 163.

88. Herodotus 8.103.

89. Hignett, *Xerxes' Invasion of Greece*, 266.

90. Herodotus 8.112.1.

CHAPTER 4. THE SECOND BURNING

1. Herodotus 8.121. Pausanias makes no mention of the Phoenician ship at Corinth, so it had probably disintegrated by the second century.

2. Pausanias 1.36.1.

3. See P. W. Wallace, "Psyttaleia and the Trophies of the Battle of Salamis," *American Journal of Archaeology* 73 (1969) 293–303; and N. G. L. Hammond, "Salamis, Attica," in R. Stillwell (ed.), *The Princeton Encyclopedia of Classical Sites* (Princeton: Princeton University Press 1976) 796.

4. Herodotus 8.123.2.

5. Herodotus 8.115.1; cf. 8.51.1.

6. Aeschylus, *Persians* 480–514; Herodotus 8.115.2–3.

7. P. Briant, *From Cyrus to Alexander: A History of the Persian Empire*, trans. P. B. Daniels (Winona Lake, IN: Eisenbrauns 2002) 530.

8. Herodotus 8.115.4.

9. Aeschylus *Persians* 800.

10. Sophocles, *Oedipus the King* 25–29. For pollution in general, see R. Parker, *Miasma: Pollution and Purification in Early Greek Religion* (Oxford: Clarendon Press 1983). Parker defines miasma as "defilement, the impairment of a thing's integrity" (pp. 3–4).

11. Herodotus 8.109.4.

12. This is the explanation for his disappearance given by J. F. Lazenby, *The Defence of Greece 490–479 BC* (Warminster: Aris and Phillips 1993) 209–10. Diodorus Siculus 11.27.3 claims that when the Athenians found out that Themistocles had accepted gifts from the Spartans, they stripped him of his generalship and replaced him by Xanthippus.

13. Briant, *From Cyrus to Alexander*, 532.

14. Herodotus 8.136.2.

15. Green, *The Greco-Persian Wars*, 222.

16. Another possibility is Building F, which formed an architectural unit with the Old Bouleutērion and which perhaps served as a state dining room. I am grateful to an anonymous reader for this suggestion.

17. Herodotus 8.140 α–β.

18. Herodotus 8.142.4.

19. Herodotus 8.143.2.

20. Herodotus 8.144.

21. C. Hignett, *Xerxes' Invasion of Greece* (Oxford: Clarendon Press 1963) 495.

22. Herodotus 9.3.1.

23. Herodotus 9.3.2.

24. Herodotus 9.6.

25. Thucydides 1.89.3.

26. See Demosthenes, *On the Crown* 204, where the victim's name is given as Cyrsilus; Lycurgus, *Against Leocrates* 122, who cites a decree condemning the victim to death; and Cicero, *On Duties* 3.11.48, situating the incident in 480, who states that Cyrsilus's proposal "violated moral principle."

27. Herodotus 9.13.2; cf. Diodorus Siculus 11.28.6.

28. Thucydides 1.89.3.

29. Herodotus 9.65.

30. So Green, *The Greco-Persian Wars*, 234, citing Herodotus 9.39.2, who indicates that the Greeks were conveying large quantities of their commissariat from the Peloponnese immediately before the Battle of Plataea.

31. Lycurgus, *Against Leocrates* 81.

32. Felix Jacoby (ed.), *Die Fragmente der griechischen Historiker (FGrH)* 115 F 153.

33. P. A. Cartledge, *After Thermopylae: The Oath of Plataea and the End of the Graeco-Persian Wars* (Oxford: Oxford University Press 2013) 4. However, Peter Krentz, "The Oath of Marathon, not Plataea," *Hesperia* 76 (2007) 731–42, makes a case for the Athenians taking the oath in 490. See, too, D. L. Kellogg, "The Place of Publication of the Ephebic Oath and the 'Oath of Plataia,'" *Hesperia* 82 (2013) 263–76, who also argues for the earlier date.

34. P. Siewert, *Der Eid von Plataia* (Munich: C. H. Beck 1972).

35. See most recently J. Hall, *Artifact and Artifice: Classical Archaeology and the Ancient Historian* (Chicago: Chicago University Press 2014) 55–76.

36. Herodotus (7.132.2) mentions an earlier oath that was taken by all the Greeks in 480 in accordance with which those who medized would be forced to pay a tithe to Delphi once the Persians had been defeated.

37. Herodotus 9.31–32.

38. Herodotus 9.70.1–2.

39. Herodotus 9.77.

40. Herodotus 9.82.3.

41. Herodotus 9.100.

42. Herodotus 8.131.1.

43. Thucydides 1.90.3; cf. Diodorus Siculus 11.40.1.

44. Thucydides 1.93.2.

45. The technical English term for this debris is "Persian destruction deposit." See K. M. Lynch, *The Symposium in Context: Pottery from a Late Archaic House near the Athenian Agora, Hesperia* suppl. 46 (Princeton: American School of Classical Studies at Athens 2011) 20–21.

46. R. A. Tomlinson, *Greek Sanctuaries* (New York: St. Martin's Press 1976) 82.

47. B. Ridgway, *Severe Style in Greek Sculpture* (Princeton: Princeton University Press 1970) 3, believes, however, that some of the sculptures were still lying around in 438 BCE.

48. Pausanias 1.27.6.

49. The French archaeologist Charles Ernest Beulé was the first to excavate the Perserschutt between 1863 and 1866. More sculptures were discovered in 1885–90 by a Greek-German team headed by Panayiotis Kavvadias, Wilhelm Dörpfeld, and Georg Kawerau. See A. Lindenlauf, "Der Perserschutt auf der Athener Akropolis," in W. Hoepfner (ed.), *Kult und Kultbauten auf der Akropolis* (Berlin: Archäologisches Seminar der Freien Universität Berlin 1997) 45–115; M. Steskal, *Der Zerstörungsbefund 480/79 der Athener Akropolis. Eine Fallstudie zum etablierten Chronologiegerüst, Antiquitates—Archäologische Forschungsergebnisse* (Hamburg: Kovač, 2004); and A. Stewart, "The Persian and Carthaginian Invasions of 480 BCE and the Beginning of the Classical Styles: Part 1, the Stratigraphy, Chronology, and Significance of the Acropolis Deposits," *American Journal of Archaeology* 112 (2008) 377–412.

50. Lynch, *The Symposium in Context*, 27.

51. Diodorus Siculus 11.41.2 and Plutarch, *Themistocles* 19.2. Work perhaps resumed in 477/6. See R. S. J. Garland, *The Piraeus: From the Fifth to the First Century BC*, 2nd ed. (London: Bristol Classical Press 2001) 14–22 and 163–65.

52. Diodorus Siculus 11.36. See further Briant, *Cyrus to Alexander*, 534–35, 540–41, and 554–55.

53. Herodotus 7.19.2.

54. J. W. I. Lee, *The Persians* (Chantilly, VA: The Great Courses 2012) 240, compares the state of mind of Persian veterans to that of American soldiers returning from Vietnam and of Soviet soldiers returning from Afghanistan in the 1980s.

CHAPTER 5. THE POSTWAR PERIOD

1. V. D. Hanson, *Carnage and Culture: Landmark Battles in the Rise of Western Power* (New York: Doubleday 2001) 35.

2. *Anabasis* 1.7.6.

3. P. Briant, *From Cyrus to Alexander: A History of the Persian Empire*, trans. P. T. Daniels (Winona Lake, IN: Eisenbrauns 2002) 515, states, "The reigns of Xerxes and his successors cannot be reduced to the ups and downs of Persian battles with Athens in the Aegean Sea."

4. A. Kuhrt, *The Persian Empire: A Corpus of Sources from the Achaemenid Period* (London: Routledge), 1:239.

5. Dio Chrysostom 11.149.

6. Thucydides 1.100.2; Diodorus Siculus 11.62.2.

7. Ctesias, *Persika*, in Felix Jacoby (ed.), *Die Fragmente der griechischen Historiker* (*FGrH*) 688 F 13 and 14; Aristotle, *Politics* 5.1311b; Diodorus Siculus 11.69, 71; Justin 3.1.

8. Kuhrt, *The Persian Empire*, 1: no. 90 (p. 306).

9. Kuhrt in "Reassessing the Reign of Xerxes in the Light of New Evidence" in M. Kozuh, W. F. M. Henkelman, C. E. Jones, and C. Woods (eds.), *Extraction and Control: Studies in Honor of Matthew W. Stolper*, Studies in Ancient Oriental Civilization 68 (Chicago: Oriental Institute of the University of Chicago) 169, writes, "Xerxes is emerging, more and more, as one of the most important architects of a stable and successful Persian empire."

10. Pausanias 1.33.2.

11. R. Stoneman, *Xerxes: A Persian Life* (New Haven: Yale University Press 2015), argues that it was Alexander the Great who did the most damage to Xerxes' reputation. In the Roman period Xerxes was demonized. See P. Hardie, "Roman Images of the Persian Wars," in E. Bridges, E. Hall, and P. J. Rhodes (eds.), *Cultural Responses to the Persian Wars: Antiquity to the Third Millennium* (Oxford: Oxford University Press 2007) 133–35. However, Pausanias (3.4.8), writing in the second century, describes Xerxes as "the king who demonstrated the greatest pride and achieved the most brilliant exploits of all who ruled over the Medes and later over the Persians."

12. Herodotus 8.109.3. Cf. also 7.24.

13. Herodotus 9.116–20.

14. P. J. Rhodes, "The impact of the Persian Wars on Classical Greece" in E. Bridges, E. Hall, and P. J. Rhodes (eds.), *Cultural Responses to the Persian Wars: Antiquity to the Third Millennium* (Oxford: Oxford University Press 2007) 34.

15. Thucydides 1.69.5. Though this observation is *parti pris*, it is still a judicious explanation for the Greek victory overall.

16. Isocrates, 4 *Panegyric* 157; Plutarch, *Aristides* 10.6.

17. R. Osborne, *Greece in the Making, 1200–479 BC*, 2nd ed. (London: Routledge 2009) 343.

18. Thucydides 1.94–96.

19. R. A. Tomlinson, *Greek Sanctuaries* (New York: St. Martin's Press 1976) 61.

20. Aeschylus, *Persians* 447–79; Suda s.v. *haliplanktos*. See further R. S. J. Garland, *Introducing New Gods: The Politics of Athenian Religion* (Ithaca: Cornell University Press 1992) 51–54; R. Parker, *Athenian Religion: A History* (Oxford: Oxford University Press 1996) 163–68.

21. *Palatine Anthology* 16.232.

22. Herodotus 7.189. See Parker, *Athenian Religion*, 156–57, for the prominence of Oreithyia in art and literature in the half-century following the Battle of Artemisium.

23. Plutarch, *Moral Precepts* 349f.

24. Garland, *Introducing New Gods*, 57.

25. Parker, *Athenian Religion*, 187.

26. Pausanias 1.14.5.

27. Plutarch, *Themistocles* 22.1; Plutarch, *Moral Precepts* 869c–d.

28. For Artemis Aristoboule, see Garland, *Introducing New Gods*, 73–78.

29. Plutarch, *Themistocles* 1.3.

30. Pausanias 2.31.7. See K. Arafat, "Records of Hate: Pausanias and the Persians," in K. Buraselis and E. Koulakiotis (eds.), *Marathon the Day After: Symposium Proceedings, Delphi 2–4 July 2010* (Athens: European Cultural Centre of Delphi 2013) 201–16.

31. Pausanias 2.31.5.

32. Thucydides 2.27.

33. V. Hanson, *Carnage and Culture*, 35.

34. For the later career and flight of Themistocles, see P. J. Rhodes, "The Athenian Revolution," in D. M. Lewis, J. Boardman, J. K. Davies, and M. Ostwald (eds.), *Cambridge Ancient History*, 2nd ed. vol. 5: *The Fifth Century BC* (Cambridge: Cambridge University Press 1992) 62–67.

35. Thucydides 1.135.2; Diodorus Siculus 11.54.2–5; Plutarch, *Themistocles* 22.3. See J. F. Lazenby, *The Defence of Greece, 490–479 BC* (Warminster: Aris and Phillips 1993) 202.

36. Plutarch, *Themistocles* 18.3.

37. Thucydides 138.2.

38. P. W. Wallace, "The Tomb of Themistokles in the Peiraieus," *Hesperia* 41 (1972) 451–62; and R. S. J. Garland, *The Piraeus: From the Fifth to the First Century BC*, 2nd ed. (London: Bristol Classical Press 2001), 147–48.

39. R. L. Lenardon, *The Saga of Themistocles* (London: Thames and Hudson 1978) 206.

40. Scholion on Aristides 3 p. 535 (Dindorf 1829).

41. J. M. Camp, *The Archaeology of Athens* (New Haven: Yale University Press 2001) 68–69.

42. Pausanias 1.28.2.

43. A. E. Raubitschek and G. P. Stevens, "The Pedestal of the Athena Promachos," *Hesperia* 15 (1946) 107–14.

44. Pausanias 10.35-2-3.

45. J. Boardman, *The Archaeology of Nostalgia: How the Greeks Re-created Their Mythical Past* (London 2002) 77.

46. The earliest references to the peace are of fourth-century date. The historian Theopompus deemed it a forgery, and it remains a controversial topic among scholars. In support of its existence, see G. Cawkwell, *The Greek Wars: The Failure of Persia* (Oxford: Oxford University Press 2005) appendix 7 (pp. 281–87). T. Hölscher, "Penelope für Persepolis: oder wie man einen Krieg gegen den Erzfeind beendet," *Jahrbuch des Deutschen Archäologischen Instituts* 126 (2011) 33–76, suggests that a Greek sculpture of a seated woman discovered at Persepolis was a diplomatic gift intended to solidify the peace. However, J. Boardman, *The Greeks in Asia* (London: Thames and Hudson 2015) pl. 6, suggests it was a gift from a subject Greek state.

47. Tomlinson, *Greek Sanctuaries*, 83.

48. Camp, *The Archaeology of Athens*, 79.

49. A. Stewart, *Classical Greece and the Birth of Western Art* (Cambridge: Cambridge University Press 2008), 140.

50. K. Arafat, "Records of Hate: Pausanias and the Persians," 214.

51. Tomlinson, *Greek Sanctuaries*, 84.

52. *Inscriptiones Graecae* (*IG*) I³ 258–72. See most recently M. B. Miles, "The Lapis Primus and the Older Parthenon," *Hesperia* 80 (2011) 657–75.

53. For the extent to which Aeschylus may have "modeled" his play on Phrynichus's *Phoenician Women*, see Anthony Podlecki, *Aeschylus: The Persians* (London: Bristol Classical Press 1991) 8–9.

54. Hypothesis to Aeschylus, *Persians*.

55. Pindar frags. 64 and 65, in C. M. Bowra, *Pindari Carmina cum Fragmentis*, 2nd ed. (Oxford: Clarendon Press 1947).

56. Simonides frags. 532–36, in D. L. Page (ed.), *Poetae Melici Graeci* (Oxford: Clarendon Press 1962), and M. L. West, *Iambi et Elegi Graeci ante Alexandrum Cantati*, 2nd ed., vol. 2 (Oxford: Clarendon Press 1992) 114.

57. *Life of Aeschylus* 18. For a useful summary of the main issues in the play, see D. Rosenbloom, "Aeschylus: *Persians*," in H. M. Roisman, *The Encyclopedia of Greek Tragedy* (Oxford: Wiley-Blackwell 2014) 1:46–54.

58. O. Broneer, "The Tent of Xerxes and the Greek Theater," *University of California Publications in Classical Archaeology* 1 (1944), 305–12, suggests that Xerxes' captured tent served as a backdrop to the production of Aeschylus's *Persians* in the Theater of Dionysus.

59. Aeschylus, *Persians* 347–49.

60. M. Gagarin, *Aeschylean Drama* (Berkeley: University of California Press 1976) 34.

61. Aeschylus, *Persians* 398–405.

62. Aeschylus, *Persians* 424–32. C. B. R. Pelling, "Aeschylus' *Persae* and History," in C. B. R. Pelling (ed.), *Greek Tragedy and the Historian* (Oxford: Oxford University Press 1997) 1–19, argues that Aeschylus is seeking to encourage his audience to acknowledge its identity as a compassionate society.

63. Aeschylus, *Persians* 470, 510–11, 548–49, 728.

64. Aeschylus, *Persians* 584–94.

65. References in Aeschylus's *Persians* to Xerxes' state of mind include: "sickness of wits" (l. 750), "hubris and a godless mind" (l. 808), "hubris" (l. 821), and "excessive daring" (l. 831). The chorus describes Darius as "revered, omnipotent, blameless, unconquerable, and equal to the gods" (854–56).

66. Varied arguments are put forward. E. Hall, *Inventing the Barbarian* (Oxford: Clarendon Press 1989) 76–100) concludes (p. 100), "Aeschylus presents Persian characteristics as vices exactly correlative to the cardinal democratic Athenian virtues." M. Griffith, "The Rule of the Father in *Persians*," in M. Lloyd (ed.), *Aeschylus: Oxford Readings in Classical Studies* (Oxford: Oxford University Press 2007) 111, writes, "In general, the racist and ethnic stereotypes of the 'Persian' or 'Asian' seem to have been much less deeply imprinted on Greek minds (at least at this early date) than the British or North American racist fantasies of the nineteenth and twentieth centuries."

67. C. Tuplin, *Achaemenid Studies, Historia* Einzelschriften 99 (Stuttgart: Franz Steiner 1996) 134.

68. E. Hall, "Aeschylus' *Persians* and Images of Islam," in E. Bridges, E. Hall, and P. J. Rhodes (eds.), *Cultural Responses to the Persian Wars* (Oxford: Oxford University Press 2007) 170–71.

69. E. Csapo and P. Wilson, "Timotheus the New Musician," in F. Budelmann (ed.), *The Cambridge Companion to Greek Lyric* (Cambridge: Cambridge University Press 2009) 288. For the text, see J. H. Hordern, *The Fragments of Timotheus* (Oxford: Oxford University Press 2002), frags. 788–91. For the shipwrecked Persian, see frag. 791 ll. 40–85.

70. M. Miller, *Athens and Persia in the Fifth Century BC: A Study in Cultural Receptivity* (Cambridge: Cambridge University Press 1997) i.

71. M. Miller, "Greece 1: Greco-Persian Cultural Relations," in E. Yarshater (ed.), *Encyclopaedia Iranica*, vol. 11 (2003) 302.

72. J. M. Hall, "Ethnicity and Cultural Exchange," in K. A. Raaflaub and H. van Wees (eds.), *A Companion to Archaic Greece* (Oxford: Wiley-Blackwell 2009) 616–17. For Callias, see H. A. Shapiro, "Kallias Kratiou Alopekethen," *Hesperia* 51 (1982) 69–73.

73. Plutarch, *Pericles* 13.9–10). For the legend that the Odeion was inspired by Xerxes' tent, see Pausanias 1.20.4. Miller, *Athens and Persia in the Fifth Century BC*, 218–42, discusses its function and architectural origins.

74. M. C. Root, "The Parthenon Frieze and the Apadana Reliefs at Persepolis: Reassessing a Programmatic Relationship," *American Journal of Archaeology* 89 (1985) 103–20. The sculptural program of the Apadana reliefs was designed during the reign of Darius I but continued into the reign of Xerxes.

75. Miller, *Athens and Persia in the Fifth Century BC*, 240.

76. Pausanias 3.11.2–3.

77. Homer, *Iliad* 2.867. Tuplin, *Achaemenid Studies*, 133 n. 3, points out that the Carians are a special case in that they "can also be described as occupying (properly Greek?) Miletus."

78. For the word *barbaros*, see J. K. Davies, "Greece after the Persian Wars," in D. M. Lewis, J. Boardman, J. K. Davies, and M. Ostwald (eds.), *Cambridge Ancient History*, 2nd ed., vol. 5: *The Fifth Century BC* (Cambridge: Cambridge University Press 1992) 16–17.

79. Herodotus 9.11.2; cf. 9.55.2. J. M. Hall, *Ethnic Identity in Greek History* (Cambridge: Cambridge University Press 1997) 10–11, notes that we lack any data regarding the usage of the word *barbaros* for the crucial period from the middle of the sixth century to the time of Aeschylus's play.

80. M. C. Root, "Reading Persepolis in Greek: Gifts of the Yauna," in C. Tuplin (ed.), *Persian Responses: Political and Cultural Interaction with (in) the Achaemenid Empire* (Swansea: Classical Press of Wales 2007) 178. Root does not, however, endorse this view but instead points out "we might also detect a wish to create unity in diversity out of the dispersed and varied realities of being Yauna (i.e., Greek)."

81. Herodotus 7.104.4.

82. For barbarian stereotypes in tragedy, see E. Hall, *Inventing the Barbarian*, 102–13. She writes (p. 103): "The 'truths' that Thracians were boors, Egyptians charlatans and Phrygians effeminate were deemed self-evident, and came to affect the tragedians' recasting of myth; tragic drama therefore provided in its turn cultural authorization of the perpetuation of the stereotype."

83. Rhodes, "The Impact of the Persian Wars on Classical Greece," 36–38.

84. E. Hall, *Inventing the Barbarian*.

85. J. Haubold, "Xerxes' Homer," in E. Bridges, E. Hall, and P. J. Rhodes (eds.), *Cultural Responses to the Persian Wars* (Oxford: Oxford University Press: 2007) 54–61.

86. G. de Ste. Croix, *The Class Struggle in the Ancient Greek World: From the Archaic Age to the Arab Conquests* (London: Duckworth 1981) 140.

EPILOGUE

1. A. Kuhrt, *The Ancient Near East, c. 3000–330 BC* (London: Routledge) 2:681, puts it well: "As guardian of Ahuramazda's creation, ruling over 'this earth' with his aid, he himself was bound to uphold the moral-political fabric and his actions were determined by the demands of appropriate high principles. He presented himself as an embodiment of positive virtues, which fitted him to rule."

2. S. Hornblower, *The Greek World, 479–323 BC*, 4th ed. (London: Routledge 2011) 322 n. 1.

3. J. W. I. Lee, *The Persian Empire* (Chantilly, VA: The Great Courses 2012) 239.

4. http://www.economist.com/news/books-and-arts/21572740-debunking-myths
-sustained-ayatollah-khomeinis-republic-waiting-god.

5. For a history of Athens from antiquity to the modern day, see Robin Waterfield, *Athens: From Ancient Ideal to Modern City* (New York: Basic Books 2004), and Kevin Andrews, *Athens Alive: The Practical Tourist's Companion to the Fall of Man* (Athens: Hermes 1979).

6. http://www.theguardian.com/world/2014/nov/30/athens-1944-britains-dirty-secret.

A NOTE ON SOURCES

1. M. Waters, *Ancient Persia: A Concise History of the Achaemenid Empire, 550–330 BCE* (Cambridge: Cambridge University Press 2014) 120.

2. A. Kuhrt, *The Persian Empire: A Corpus of Sources from the Achaemenid Period* (London: Routledge 2010) 1:238–309, provides a list of sources, overwhelmingly Greek, relating to the reign of Xerxes.

3. Herodotus 8.121.1. E. Gruen, *The Invention of the Other* (Princeton: Princeton University Press 2011) 20, argues against the claim that the play advocates an "essentialist divide" between East and West.

4. Aeschylus, *Persians* 349.

5. Herodotus 9.63.2.

6. N. G. L. Hammond, "The Expedition of Xerxes," in J. Boardman, N. G. L. Hammond, D. M. Lewis, and M. Ostwald (eds.), *Cambridge Ancient History*, 2nd ed., vol. 4: *Persia, Greece and the Western Mediterranean, c. 525 to 479 BC* (Cambridge: Cambridge University Press 1988) 536.

7. P. Briant, *From Cyrus to Alexander: A History of the Persian Empire*, trans. P. B. Daniels (Winona Lake, IN: Eisenbrauns 2002).

8. We don't know whether Herodotus ever visited Thrace. He may have been dependent on his predecessor Hecataeus for his knowledge of this region.

9. Aeschylus, *Persians* 466–67; Herodotus 8.90.4.

10. Herodotus 6.117 (Epizelus) and 8.65 (Dikaios).

11. D. Lateiner, *The Historical Method of Herodotus* (Toronto: University of Toronto Press 1989) 152.

12. Herodotus erroneously believed that all Persian proper names ended in "s" (1.139).

13. R. V. Munson, *Herodotus: Volume 2*, Oxford Readings in Classical Studies (Oxford: Oxford University Press 2013) 329.

14. J. Haubold, "Xerxes' Homer," in E. Bridges, E. Hall, and P. J. Rhodes (eds.), *Cultural Responses to the Persian Wars* (Oxford: Oxford University Press 2007) 49–50, points out that not only Xerxes' thinking but also that of the Persians "shows signs of the rationalizing approach associated with the sophists."

15. D. M. Lewis, "Persians in Herodotus," in M. H. Jameson (ed.), *The Greek Historians: Literature and History; Papers Presented to A. E. Raubitschek* (Stanford, CA: Anma Libri 1985) 101–17, demonstrated that Herodotus must have had access to documentary texts for Persian affairs, but he says nothing of his possible sources for the narrative of Xerxes' invasion. On Herodotus's sources in general, see appendix by G. S. Shrimpton and K. M. Gillis in G. S. Shrimpton, *History and Memory in Ancient Greece* (Montreal: McGill-Queen's University Press 1997).

16. Herodotus 9.16. Herodotus did not consult the Persian himself but says he learned of the testimony from a (named) Boeotian. Interestingly, he reports that the Persian understood Greek.

17. Cf. Herodotus 8.67–69.

18. P. Green, *The Greco-Persian Wars* (Berkeley: University of California Press 1996) 88, citing Herodotus 7.114.2 (Xerxes' wife Amastris buries fourteen children alive). Herodotus also engages in "atrocity propaganda" with respect to the Athenians (9.120), however, as Donald Lateiner has pointed out to me.

19. Felix Jacoby (ed.), *Die Fragmente der griechischen Historiker (FGrH)* 688. See J. P. Stronk, *Ctesias' Persian History: Part 1, Introduction, Text, and Translation* (Düsseldorf: Wellem Verlag 2010); L. Llewellyn-Jones and J. Robson, *Ctesias' History of Persia: Tales of the Orient* (London: Routledge 2010).

20. Diodorus Siculus 2.32.4.

SUGGESTED FURTHER READING

For Herodotus I recommend Robert B. Strassler (ed.), *The Landmark Herodotus* (Pantheon Books: New York 2007), both for its numerous essays on a wide range of subjects relating to the Greco-Persian Wars written by top-notch scholars and for its 127 maps illustrating every episode in the narrative. Its introduction, written by Rosalind Thomas, is an excellent place to become acquainted with one of the most delightful minds that antiquity produced. It is not, however, the best translation, of which there have been no fewer than seven since 1987. Robin Waterfield's 1988 rendering in the Oxford World's Classics series is one of the finest. Tom Holland's 2014 translation for Viking is more colloquial and at times somewhat idiosyncratic.

Herodotus's trustworthiness as a historian is a continuing subject of controversy. One of his sternest critics is Detlev Fehling, *Herodotus and His Sources: Citation, Invention, and Narrative Art*, trans. J. G. Howie (Leeds, England: Francis Cairns 1989). One of his staunchest defenders is W. Kendrick Pritchett, *The Liar School of Herodotus* (Amsterdam: J. C. Gieben 1993). John Myres, *Herodotus: Father of History* (Oxford: Clarendon Press 1953), though dated, provides a useful assessment of Herodotus's significance as a historian. For Herodotus's style and methods, Jennifer Roberts's *Herodotus: A Very Short Introduction* (Oxford: Oxford University Press 2011) is indeed an excellent introduction. I also strongly recommend Donald Lateiner, *The Historical Method of Herodotus* (Toronto: University of Toronto Press 1989), both detailed and accessible. Rosalind Thomas, *Herodotus in Context: Ethnography, Science and the Art of Persuasion* (Cambridge: Cambridge University Press 2000), emphasizes the degree to which the historian draws on the work of medical writers, natural scientists, and sophists of the late fifth century. As she points out, he even ascribes "rather sophistic language" to Xerxes (p. 225). Among many other valuable discussions, I would single out Charles Fornara, *Herodotus: An Interpretive Essay* (Oxford: Clarendon Press 1971); John Gould, *Herodotus* (London: Weidenfeld and Nicolson 1989); François Hartog, *The Mirror of Herodotus: The Representation of the Other in the Writing of History*, trans. J. Lloyd (Berkeley: University of California Press 1988); Virginia Hunter, *Past and Process in Herodotus and Thucydides* (Princeton: Princeton University Press 1982); Henry Immerwahr, *Form and Thought in Herodotus* (Chapel Hill: American Philological Association 1966); Mabel L. Lang, *Herodotean Narrative and Discourse* (Cambridge, MA: Harvard University Press 1984);

and K. H. Waters, *Herodotus the Historian: His Problems, Method, and Originality* (Norman: University of Oklahoma Press 1985).

There are many fine translations of Aeschylus's *Persians* including Janet Lembke and C. J. Harrison, *Aeschylus: Persians* (Oxford: Oxford University Press 1991); Chris Collard, *Aeschylus' Persians and Other Plays* (Oxford: Oxford University Press 2008); Alan H. Sommerstein, *Aeschylus Persians and Other Plays* (London: Penguin Books 2009); and *Aeschylus I*, ed. Mark Griffith and Glenn W. Most, 3rd ed. (Chicago: University of Chicago Press 2013). H. D. Broadbent, *The Persae of Aeschylus* (Cambridge: Cambridge University Press 1960), gives a historical commentary on the play. David Rosenbloom, *Aeschylus: Persians* (London: Duckworth 2006), provides a useful introduction, supplemented by an account of the play's performance history.

For Thucydides, Strassler's *The Landmark Thucydides* (New York: Touchstone 1998) provides copious maps and essays. The extant portion of Timotheus's poem on Salamis is available in J. H. Hordern, *The Fragments of Timotheus of Miletus* (Oxford: Oxford University Press: 2002). For Diodorus Siculus, the best translation is Peter Green, *Diodorus Siculus Books 11–12.37.1: Greek History, 480–431 BC; The Alternative Version* (Austin: University of Texas Press 2006), which also contains many useful notes on specific passages. Plutarch's "Life of Themistocles" is most readily available in *Plutarch—The Rise and Fall of Athens: Nine Greek Lives*, trans. Ian Scott-Kilvert (London: Penguin Books 1960]).

The best introductions to the Achaemenid Empire are Amélie Kuhrt, *The Persian Empire: A Corpus of Sources from the Achaemenid Period*, pbk. ed. (New York: Routledge, 2010); and Matthew W. Waters, *Ancient Persia: A Concise History of the Achaemenid Empire, 550–330 BCE* (Cambridge: Cambridge University Press 2014). Maria Brosius, *The Persians* (London: Routledge 2006), has chapters on economy, society, gender, power, and defense. Josef Wiesehöfer, *Ancient Persia from 550 BC to 650 AD*, trans. A. Azodi (London: I. B. Tauris 1966), has an illuminating description of daily life in Achaemenid Persia. Pierre Briant, *From Cyrus to Alexander: A History of the Persian Empire*, trans. P. B. Daniels (Winona Lake, IN: Eisenbrauns 2002) is magisterial. Albert T. Olmstead, *History of the Persian Empire* (Chicago: University of Chicago Press 1959) is still useful. John W. I. Lee, *The Persian Empire* (Chantilly: Great Courses 2012), which is available either on CD or DVD, is a series of lectures on a variety of topics relating to Persia, including several on the Greco-Persian Wars.

There are a number of narrative accounts of the Greco-Persian Wars. A good place to begin is Philip de Souza's lavishly illustrated *The Greek and Persian Wars, 499–386* (Oxford: Osprey Publishing 2003). John Sharwood Smith, *Greece and the Persians* (Bristol: Bristol Classical Press 1990), offers a brief introduction both to the Persians and to Xerxes' campaign. N. Whately, "On the Possibility of Reconstructing Marathon and Other Ancient Battles," *Journal for Hellenic Studies* 84 (1964) 119–39, is valuable and accessible for all studies of war. The first scholarly investigation of Salamis is W. W. Goodwin, "The Battle of Salamis," *Harvard Studies in Classical Philology* 17 (1906) 74–101, which superseded an earlier article of his in the *Papers of the American School of*

Classical Studies 1 (1885) 239–62, followed by N. Rados, *La Bataille de Salamine* (Paris: Fontemoing & Cie 1915). Both are still useful. Among the more general accounts of the wars I particularly recommend Peter Green, *The Greco-Persian Wars* (Berkeley, CA: University of California Press 1998), which offers an admirable blend of scholarship and imagination, and J. F. Lazenby, *The Defence of Greece, 490–479 BC* (Warminster: Aris and Phillips 1993), which is thorough and painstaking. Andrew R. Burn, *Persia and the Greeks: The Defense of the West, 546–478. 2nd ed.* (Stanford: Stanford University Press 1984), is still useful, even though it has in part been superseded by more recent accounts. C. Hignett, *Xerxes' Invasion of Greece* (Oxford: Clarendon Press 1963), is particularly valuable in its discussion of the sources relating to Xerxes' campaign. Hignett gives the impression of an acute mind in constant debate with other scholars, which the nonexpert may find rather distracting. N. G. L. Hammond, "The Expedition of Xerxes," in J. Boardman, N. G. L. Hammond, D. M. Lewis, and M. Ostwald (eds.), *Cambridge Ancient History*, 2nd ed., vol. 4: *Persia, Greece and the Western Mediterranean, c. 525 to 479 BC* (Cambridge: Cambridge University Press 1988), is particularly strong on technical details relating to the march. George Cawkwell, *The Greek Wars: The Failure of Persia* (Oxford: Oxford University Press 2005), is, in the words of the blurb, more of a discussion than a narrative. Its stimulating premise is that the Persians' failure was largely of their own making and had little to do with Greek valor.

For Marathon I recommend Peter Krentz, *The Battle of Marathon* (New Haven: Yale University Press 2010), and Richard A. Billows, *Marathon: How One Battle Changed Western Civilization* (New York Overlook Duckworth 2010). Paul Cartledge, *Thermopylae: The Battle That Changed the World* (Basingstoke: Macmillan 2006), is not only thrillingly written but also contains an important discussion of the legend that the three hundred have inspired down the ages. For Salamis, H. D. Wallinga, *Xerxes' Greek Adventure: The Naval Perspective* (Leiden: Brill 2005), offers an interesting interpretation on the reasons for the invasion, plus detailed discussion of various topics, including the size of Xerxes' navy, the topography of the battlefield, and the Persian plan of attack. Barry Strauss, *The Battle of Salamis: The Naval Encounter That Saved Greece—and Western Civilization* (New York: Simon and Schuster 2004), is both lively, insightful, and informative. There is a useful chapter of Salamis in Victor D. Hanson, *Carnage and Culture: Landmark Battles in the Rise of Western Power* (New York: Doubleday 2001). Hanson argues that the battle played a major role in the evolution of the distinctively lethal Western way of waging war. Jon D. Mikalson, *Herodotus and Religion in the Persian Wars* (Chapel Hill: University of North Carolina Press 2003), demonstrates how religion shaped the Greek response to the invasion. His first chapter, "A Religious Account of the Persian Invasions," is especially valuable. Paul Cartledge, *After Thermopylae: The Oath of Plataea and the End of the Graeco-Persian Wars* (Oxford: Oxford University Press 2013) examines the knotty question as to whether the Athenians (and other Greeks) swore not to repair the temples the Persians had destroyed.

No study focuses specifically on the Persian destruction of Athens. John M. Camp, *The Archaeology of Athens* (New Haven: Yale University Press 2001) contains invaluable snippets of information about individual buildings and is well illustrated. For the aftermath to the victory John K. Davies, "Greece after the Persian Wars," pp. 15–33, in D. M. Lewis, J. Boardman, J. K. Davies, and M. Ostwald (eds.), *Cambridge Ancient History*, 2nd ed., vol. 5: *The Fifth Century BC* (Cambridge: Cambridge University Press 1992), is valuable. Margaret C. Miller, *Athens and Persia in the Fifth Century BC: A Study in Cultural Receptivity* (Cambridge: Cambridge University Press 1997), offers a detailed study of Athens's response to Persian culture in the postwar era. Emma Bridges, Edith Hall, and P. J Rhodes (eds.), *Cultural Responses to the Persian Wars: Antiquity to the Third Millennium* (Oxford: Oxford University 2007), is, as its title indicates, a collection of wide-ranging essays that demonstrate how the Greco-Persian Wars have helped shape the West's political consciousness.

The best fictional account of the Persian invasion is Tom Holland's *Persian Fire: The First World Empire and the Battle for the West* (2005), which is fast-paced and engrossing. Last but by no means least the battles have also inspired films. *The 300 Spartans*, directed by Rudolf Maté and released in 1962, depicts the famous last stand of the Spartans at the Battle of Thermopylae. It has a musical score by Manos Hadjidakis. According to Wikipedia (I have been unable to discover any other source for this), the Greek Ministry of Defense "loaned" five thousand of its military personnel to stand in as the Greeks and Persians. The film inspired the graphic artist Frank Miller to write a book of the battle, which in turn became the screenplay for a "fantasy action film" called *The 300*, directed by Zack Snyder (2007). As Jonathan Hall notes, whatever its inaccuracies, the film "offers a valuable barometer for popular perceptions of Sparta and ancient Greece more generally"—and, one might add, of modern day Iran as well.[*] Rahmin and Julian Abhari's online *Xerxes Speaks: A Graphic Novel on Greco-Persian Wars from Persian Point of View* (2014), available only in a Kindle edition, was written in response to Miller's novel, whose portrayal of the Persians they found deeply upsetting "at both the intellectual and emotional level."[†]

---

[*] J. Hall, "Delphic Vapours," in *Artifact and Artifice: Classical Archaeology and the Ancient Historian* (Chicago: University of Chicago Press 2014) 17–34 (p. 17).
[†] http://www.payvand.com/news/14/sep/1061.html. I am grateful to an anonymous reader for this reference.

INDEX

Made in United States
Orlando, FL
10 February 2023

29775629R00104